WHY DOES MY HORSE . . . ?

WHY DOES MY HORSE . . . ?

Paul McGreevy

Drawings by Stanley Burgess

Trafalgar Square Publishing

First published in the United States of America 1996 by
Trafalgar Square Publishing,
North Pomfret, Vermont 05053

**Printed in Great Britain by
Biddles Ltd, Guildford and King's Lynn**

ISBN 1–57076–067–5

Library of Congress Catalog Card Number: 96–60619

Phototypeset by Intype London Ltd

To JT
with thanks for all the tea and toast

NOTICE TO READERS

Behaviour problems of any kind in horses may have under-lying medical causes, so it is important to consult a veterinary surgeon before taking any steps to alter them. Any advice given in this book should be discussed with the veterinary surgeon before being followed only with his or her complete agreement. A horse is capable of inflicting severe injury, and the measures suggested here should in any event only be used by an experienced horse-owner fully trained in horsemanship.

The Publisher makes no representation express or implied with regard to the advice contained in this book, and legal responsibility or liability cannot be accepted by the Author or Publisher for any errors or omissions that may be made or for any loss, damage, injury or problems suffered or in any way arising from the use of the methods described.

CONTENTS

ACKNOWLEDGEMENTS

Firstly, I must thank Bella, Bisto, Jessie, Mac, Bruce, Drake and Missie (pictured on the jacket) and all the other horses I have worked with in England and Australia. They have all put up with my ignorance and bluntness while patiently teaching me that one can never stop learning about this most wonderful species.

Dr Claire Weekes, Dr Anne McBride, Dr David Evans and Moistine Marsh have offered invaluable comments on the early manuscripts of this book. In addition, my colleagues in the Association of Pet Behaviour Counsellors, John Fisher and Sarah Heath, have provided welcome support and advice. The structure of their books *Why Does My Dog . . . ?* and *Why Does My Cat . . . ?* has formed the framework for this one.

With his cartoons, Dr Stan Burgess, a former primary school-mate of mine and more recently a colleague and great friend at Bristol University, has supplied a welcome injection of humour. I am also indebted to my fellow researchers at Bristol's veterinary school, Christine Nicol, Roy Jones and Cecilia Lindberg, for providing me with an insight into the importance of behaviour in our understanding of horse welfare. Lucy Rees, Bonny Williams, Gerald Downes, Greg Kirk, Nikki Reeves and Terry Waide also deserve thanks for the formal and informal tuition in equitation and horsemanship that they have given me over the years. Michael Lutteral has generously allowed me to use his fax machine for transhemispheric correspondence with my ever-patient publisher.

Finally, I would like to thank my friends and family for their enthusiasm and tolerance during the writing of this book.

Part One

BEHAVIOUR THERAPY FOR HORSES

1

MISUNDERSTANDINGS AND 'MISBEHAVIOUR'

This book deals with unwelcome equine behaviours as well as normal ones. For the horse, less desirable activities are often signs of fear and frustration; for humans, they are often a *source* of fear and frustration. We owe it to our horses to examine their 'misbehaviour' in order to overcome our misunderstandings, because misunderstandings represent barriers between humans and horses. These barriers arise whenever man uses horses, and there will be a need for a book like this as long as man and horse remain companions.

There are, of course, countless examples of excellent bonds between humans and horses, but let's start by having a quick look at some barriers. Let me take you to an imaginary horse show and gymkhana on a hazy August afternoon. It could be anywhere in the world, but you'll notice how terribly well spoken the chap in the public address caravan is, so let's assume we're somewhere in the English Home Counties! There are roped-in enclosures, burger vans, coloured fences and judges in floppy hats, and all around us are horses and ponies. First we see them being unloaded from their horse boxes, groomed, tacked up and warmed up. Then, as their riders compete with one another, they are asked to perform. Finally, they are untacked, groomed and loaded in preparation for their trip home.

At every step in this process, we can spot humans who feel that their equine friends are not behaving perfectly. One bay gelding fidgets while being groomed and a grey mare bites her rider as she is being girthed up. Several chubby ponies don't move fast enough, three or four others won't jump fences and an unmistakably thready scream tells us that a third group are refusing to stop galloping. If we wait long enough we will see the sun set as a young cob refuses to walk into his trailer at the eighty-fifth attempt.

All of these imperfections in behaviour will have been greeted with a variety of curses. However, humans rarely choose mere cursing as a means of changing an animal's behaviour. They prefer to act – and that is why, at the same show, we'll see people kicking flanks, whipping quarters and yanking on reins. They believe that they have 'problem horses', which implies that the horses are to blame. It would be much fairer, though, to say that the horses have acquired unwelcome behaviour patterns. Humans often express their frustration by 'disciplining' the culprits, but disciplinary measures are rarely understood by horses because they rarely involve a consideration of how horses think. I believe that by learning how a horse thinks and what motivates him, we can use more enlightened methods to achieve the behaviours we prefer.

Horses resent demonstrations of authority. They have evolved to recognise rank only in disputes over resources like food and water. They normally avoid aversive or unpleasant situations and are extremely wary of predators – their greatest fear is to be trapped by another creature. The importance of this survival trait is illustrated by the fact that thousands of years of selective breeding have done very little to eliminate it from the behavioural repertoire. Horses do everything they can to maximise their chances of survival. The bolting ponies which provoked the screams at our imaginary show may have been startled by the movement of a dog lurking under a horse box. Since they cannot know for sure that wolves are no longer indigenous to the British Isles, they take appropriate steps to avoid being eaten.

So, to find our way into horses' minds, we have to recall their origins in the process of evolution. Bearing in mind that early man used horses as a food source, we should acknowledge how tolerant horses are to put up with having a potential predator on their backs, bearing this burden even when it becomes a source of pain. Now imagine, if you will, a time-travelling caveman turning up at our twentieth-century horse show. He has suddenly appeared, between the show secretary's trestle table and the hot-dog wagon, armed with a prehistoric cannon bone. How amazed he would be to see his descendants riding around on dutiful Thorough-breds, jumping ornamental gates and smiling at the judges. Those who rode without displays of nervousness, frustration or temper and without using their weapons would particularly impress him.

Our freshly beamed-down Neanderthal would not know whether the human handlers and riders were also 'owners', and this should prompt us to consider how horses regard humans. Since with this book we are aiming to dismantle barriers from both the human and the equine perspective, we should remember that the concept of ownership means nothing to a horse. From a horse's point of view there are two sorts of human: riders and handlers. Riders provide instructions, praise and punishment. Handlers supply food, grooming and companionship. These days more and more riders are also handlers. For the sake of simplicity I have assumed that readers of this book play both roles, and so we will address problems encountered both from the horse's back and from the ground.

Clearly, humans provide both good and bad things in a horse's life. And for the horse, it is a question not only of *who* provides these things but also of *how* they are provided. Horses learn by association, and they have terrific memory. This memory is especially finely tuned, it seems, for things they regard as threatening – an excellent characteristic to have if you are an animal that is considered delicious by carnivores! As we shall see throughout this book, these strong negative associations are often at play when problems arise. Take as an example a horse's predisposition to associate punishment with the presence of the human delivering it rather than with the inappropriate behaviour that it has just performed. While the misbehaviour persists, the misunderstanding provokes the horse to defend itself against humans in the future. The result is learned aggression.

Of the problem cases I deal with almost a third involve horses that show, amongst other characteristics, learned aggression. A revealing example is Annie, a two-year-old home-bred filly who had been orphaned at four weeks of age and had since been raised by her devoted owner, Miss Harris. Annie was referred to me by her veterinary surgeon, who explained that she had been aggressive to humans for the last six months, and the problem had become steadily worse.

The aggression had reached the point where Miss Harris could not enter the stable if Annie was inside. The stable door opened into Annie's paddock and remained open all of the time. Without any equine company or competition, Annie's reign over stable and field was supreme. Miss Harris's boyfriend, a committed socialist who disliked horses almost as much as he did Tories, referred to Annie as the Iron Maiden. Everyone seemed to be frightened of the filly and no one would help Miss Harris with her *enfant terrible.* Mucking out the stable involved bribes and distractions. Miss Harris would spy out her moment, scurry to the far end of the field, scatter some pony nuts and then run like blazes away from the advancing gnashing teeth. Only when Annie was fully occupied with foraging for the nuts would her distraught owner feel courageous enough to enter the stable and tidy up the bedding. Despite the hopes that she had entertained of one day competing with Annie the Orphan, Miss Harris was considering sending her to a youngstock sale.

When I examined the unwelcome behaviour, I rapidly established the gravity of the situation and realised that the owner's misery was compounded by her sense of being betrayed by her equine dependant. Miss Harris gave me a detailed account of what had happened the first time she detected the problem. It had been during Annie's second winter when she was about eighteen months old; she was growing rapidly and had a ravenous appetite. On a particularly cold February evening, Miss Harris had been delayed in getting away from her office and was in a rush to get ready for an evening out. Annie's evening feed was prepared and brought to her stable. Conscious of her boyfriend's insistence that she should not be late, Miss Harris had attempted to make up time by grooming the filly while she was eating. Annie had thrust her head up out of the bucket and grimaced at her owner before biting her arm. Miss Harris told me that she had been outraged. She had raced out of the stable, opened the tack room, removed a schooling-whip and returned to give her filly the belting she felt she deserved. With self-righteous indignation she whipped the horse on the quarters and was instantly floored by a double-barrelled kick to the chest. Winded and thoroughly depressed, she had picked herself up and driven home leaving Annie to eat the remains of her meal.

As Miss Harris recounted subsequent episodes, it became clear to me that the main problem had been repeated exclusively in the stable, at feeding time. I explained to her how I thought Annie had viewed the initial incident. Having had to wait for her supper, the filly was particularly motivated to eat when the food eventually appeared. When her handler unwittingly disturbed her by starting to groom her, Annie simply protected this valuable resource by trying to scare off what she perceived as possible competition. The warning grimace failed to work, so Annie followed through with a bite – which was resoundingly effective. The competition had been won and the opponent retreated. In a separate incident, a short time later, as she continued to munch her cereal Annie was attacked by Miss Harris from behind. Annie defended herself successfully but learned to be wary of unprovoked attacks from behind by her only human companion.

She probably remembered two things from the evening's events. Firstly, she could get undisturbed access to tasty meals if she bit the human who had just delivered them. Secondly, she had learned that she should never get cornered by Miss Harris, who was likely to whip her without warning. The stable had become the focus of the learned aggression because that was where the best meals were repeatedly relinquished by her human companion. The increasingly frequent displays of learned aggression around food were met with increasing attempts to instil discipline. Miss Harris had become so nervous that she had shown the filly the whip every time she entered the loose-box. Thus, misunderstandings had broken the bond that had existed between horse and human; the barriers were in place. Punishment was clearly making matters worse, so we decided to use a programme of behavioural therapy to break down those barriers.

Annie did not go to the youngstock sale. Instead, she travelled to a livery yard where there was a number of mares and geldings of different ages. This was the most important step in the programme that we adopted to modify her behaviour. The move provided Annie not only with equine peers for the first time in her life, but also with an array of buildings none of which had any prior associations for her. We agreed that she should be fed in a variety of different contexts so that none would become particularly associated with food, and that she should be left alone to eat for the first two weeks of the programme. At no point was she to see humans backing away from the food: it was simply to be available in the box when she entered it. The idea was to break down both the associations that she had built up with food and her way of defending it.

Next, we wanted to return to a situation where the filly could be groomed while eating. To achieve this, it was important to reward the behaviour that we required. Miss Harris did this with the help of another owner on the yard, who gave Annie small food rewards from a bucket when she stood quietly to be groomed. For the first month this was done outside, and then they gradually moved into the stable. Annie made remarkable progress, and a different kind of bond has now developed between the horse and the human. It is good to know that the pain-free behaviour modification programme has worked in the stable and that it will also pay dividends in Annie's future dressage career.

Learned aggression does not arise in horses while they are being ridden, but other negative associations regularly appear. The application of punishment is an intriguing part of equitation. In most cases, especially when human judgement and temper come into play, the timing of such negative stimuli is far from perfect. This is why the use of whips by children is often questioned by adult observers, who know that some little people have very big tempers! For some horses and ponies, just being aware that their rider is carrying a whip is sufficient to make them more biddable. But for those who are actually hit it is worth asking what associations a horse makes with the pain.

We all know that flogging a dead horse is a futile exercise – but then so is flogging any horse that is not able to respond as required. Not being able to respond can include *not knowing* the desired response as well as not being physically capable of performing the desired response. Obviously, if a fence is too big for a horse to jump, it is not made any more surmountable if the animal is being hit.

Punishment can come in many guises – not just 'floggings'

– and all of them are stimuli or situations that any sensible creature will avoid. Consider the example of a horse that is bolting from a car that has just back-fired. Hitting him will obviously only make him run away faster. So the instinctive response of most riders with any regard for their personal safety is to pull on the reins, and often with considerable force. However, the bolting horse may be so scared that the pain of a bit in his mouth simply confirms his fears about the unpleasantness of the situation he is in. When it becomes even more unpleasant, he does more of what comes naturally – more running away. This is why pulling on the reins can be so counter-productive.

Behaviour therapy and punishment are not the only ways in which we can modify a horse's behaviour: drugs and surgery may also be used. Both offer rapid resolutions, and yet both have their drawbacks. Drugs can have unpleasant side-effects which, in the case of those that work on the brain, can be difficult to detect. And pharmaceutical approaches to behaviour modification require more pro-longed use and are often very costly. At the moment researchers in the United States are testing drugs designed to eliminate 'stable vices' like crib-biting. So far the effects of these drugs are very short-lived, and so they would have to be administered daily at considerable expense to owners. They may also affect the horse's ability to cope with stress of a more general nature. Furthermore, since many scientists believe that 'stereotypies' (a better name for vices) are actu-ally indicators of unsuitable management, this approach to the problem is short-sighted because it removes the symp-tom, not the cause.

The other approach to crib-biting involves surgery to remove the muscles and nerves that make the behaviour possible. Although this operation has been radically modi-fied so that it is no longer as disfiguring as it once was, it has limited success. From a welfare point of view, the therapy is unattractive because it involves the risk and unpleasant-ness of a general anaesthetic and the pain of wound-healing, and because it too removes the symptom and not the cause. It effectively serves to sweep the issue of horse welfare under the carpet of convenience.

As we shall see throughout the following pages, an under-standing of equine behaviour can give us an insight into what we regard as abnormal behaviour. Given the absence of brain damage, there is usually an excellent reason for a horse behaving in a particular way – even though it may make us humans tear our hair!

This book answers sixty questions that have arisen in the stable, in the field and in the saddle, and resolves some of the fundamental misunderstandings between horses and humans. Its aim is to minimise the prevalence of problems. It does so, on the one hand, by reducing human frustration and, on the other, by reducing equine fear. We have a moral obligation to understand the needs of horses and treat them with compassion. Only by understanding what motivates them can we alter their behaviour. It is worth pointing out at this stage that horses appear to be free of some of the more complex and unpleasant motives that humans possess. Horses do not 'show people up' or 'try it on'. Neither do they 'take the mickey' out of their equine companions, so why should we imagine that they reserve humiliation for us?

What follows is not meant to be a complete account of horse behaviour. That book has not been written, and I doubt that it ever could be. *Why Does My Horse . . .?* will have served its purpose if it encourages anyone who enjoys being around horses to do so with a greater understanding of the horse's mind. It may also help all of us to understand *why* we enjoy being around horses, and even prompt further reading and research. There are many fascinating areas of horse behaviour that will remain mysteries and continue to puzzle us. Although many of the examples used in the book refer to an English setting, it is hoped that the principles they illustrate can be applied worldwide.

Ultimately, we would do well to remember that horses do not automatically understand human behaviour any better than we understand theirs. But we are the ones who can work to improve mutual respect and understanding. We can learn a great deal from our own experiences, and *Why Does My Horse . . .?* is designed to help the process along. So read on, trot on and enjoy!

2

WHAT AFFECTS BEHAVIOUR?

Of course, horses are not robots. They have feelings, moods and personalities. However, there are similarities between the behaviour of horses and that of machines. A robot responds to a given set of information according to the way in which it has been programmed. A horse's behaviour has also been programmed – by evolution, selective breeding and the individual's previous experience. The set of information that he is given comes from his field-mates, his rider, his stable and, in fact, everything in his environment. Therefore, to have a clear understanding of why horses do what they do we must consider the effects of numerous factors in their lives, and indeed, in both their species and their individual development. The object of this chapter is to illustrate the myriad ingredients that influence equine behaviour. Only by paying attention to these can we truly get to know the individual characteristics of the animals that occupy not only our stables but also an important place in our hearts and in our culture.

GENETICS

Just as people of different ethnic origins have diverse languages, body shape, colour, stature and disparate tastes in food, so horses have sizes, shapes and behaviours that are exhibited to a greater degree in one breed than in another. Genes, in conjunction with environmental influences, determine how our horses look and behave. This interaction between genetics and the environment occurs naturally; it is known as *natural selection* and is the basis for evolution, as we shall see when we consider horse *types*. The term *artificial selection* describes the process by which man can influence the genetic make-up of animals. By selectively breeding for favoured bloodlines, we can speed up the process of developing different groups of horses that breed true. These groups are the *breeds*. Just as with people of a different nation, horses of different breeds show characteristics that are common to a *family group*.

Type

Environmental features of a region, such as the climate and the landscape, foster the development of certain behavioural traits and conformational features which improve the survival chances of resident animals. We can see this effect in the two recognised horse types: the so-called 'warm-blooded' horses (exemplified by the Arab) and the 'cold-blooded' ones (such as the Shire). These terms do not actually refer to the horses' blood heat but are general labels for their body shapes, temperaments and climatic origins. In fact, it is known that the skin can be maintained at a constant temperature even though the climatic temperature may vary. Warm-bloods can tolerate changes in the air temperature in the range +5°C to +30° C (37°F to 86°F), while for cold-bloods the range is from −10° C to +20° C (15°F to 68°F).

The cold-bloods developed in the cooler habitats of Europe and Northwest Asia, while the warm-bloods have their ancestral homes in hot, dry regions close to the equator. Thus, an archetypal cold-blood is equipped with a chunky body in order to reduce heat loss, a tendency to increase body weight in times of plenty by the deposition of subcutaneous fat, and the capacity to grow a very thick winter coat. He is the one with a phlegmatic temperament. The warm-blood, on the other hand, is behaviourally more reactive, or flighty, in that he tends to respond to more subtle stimuli. He has a thinner skin than his cool country cousin and his athletic physique more rapidly turns to a bag of bones when exposed to hard times.

The build of a cold-blood befits the terrain that his ancestors encountered in the wetter northern territories such as the steppes of Russia. Having to plod through bogs and marshes demanded the strength of heavy-boned legs and muscles to match. However, in habitats such as the semi-desert, at the other end of the climatic spectrum, the long distances between water sources and areas of good grazing meant that sheer endurance was more of an aid to survival. Just as the narrow tyres of a racing bike maximise performance in a velodrome while those fitted to a mountain bike are more suitable for variable terrain, the finer legs and smaller hooves found in warm-blooded horses are more efficient for sustained work on the harder ground of semi-desert habitats.

The debate continues as to when the process of domestication first began for the horse, and fresh archaeological evidence is continually being uncovered to add to the discussion. Bit wear on the molars of horse skulls that date back to 6000 BC is thought by some to mark the first use of horses as riding animals. However, this assumption fails to address the possibility that before that time horses were ridden in bitless bridles. Whatever the date of the first-ever riding lesson, as herbivores with large muscle masses early domesticated horses probably first found their way into man's domain by virtue of their appeal as meat animals. It is also possible that, rather than being simply harvested from the wild, these animals were penned up or housed. Evidence of their having been housed dates back to 2000 BC, since skulls from this time have been shown to bear signs of crib-biting, which is thought to arise only in confined animals.

So, starting with warm- and cold-blooded types that had adapted the species to different habitats, man has selectively bred horses for a variety of behavioural traits. Taking any indigenous type as his raw material, he was also able to select different sizes and shapes for different kinds of work. The Arab and the shire perfectly illustrate the diversity in the origins of the domestic horses we see today. Both breeds have been finely selected by man, thereby grossly exaggerating conformational differences. It is said that the Shire was initially the product of intensive breeding for a massive war-horse capable of carrying heavily armoured knights into battle, while the cultural importance of the Arabian horse in the Middle East highlights the value to Bedouins of an animal that had been bred to cope with extended journeys from one camp to another.

The numerous breeds are usually described as being either horses or ponies. Before considering the differences between the two, it is worth emphasising that they are more or less variations on the same theme, except that there is a height limit of 14.2 hands (148 cm (58 ins) from the ground to the withers) below which an equine is referred to as a pony. Between ponies and horses we find 'cobs', which are often regarded as combining the best features of both ends of the market. Being over 14.2 hands but having the sturdy build that one expects in a pony, as occupants of the middle ground between horses and ponies cobs help to confirm that the distinction between the first two is largely a semantic one. As if to highlight the fact that 14.2 hands is only an arbitrary cut-off point, afficionados of certain breeds completely ignore the distance from the animal's withers to the ground. Hence one never encounters such a thing as an Arab pony or a Polo horse. Similarly, we are told that the Falabella breed is technically a horse even though it stands, on average, around 75 cm (30 ins) high.

The main differences found in ponies when we compare them with horses are to do with the body shape and metabolism that accompany being short-legged. The equine digestive system relies on a glorified rotting process involving bugs in the large bowel. This decomposition is called 'hind-gut fermentation'. Because the hind-gut is so important for the breakdown of food, it is especially large in pony breeds that have had to make the most of limited resources, such as the Shetland pony which in its Scottish homeland often resorts to seaweed for nutrition. This comparative increase in the ratio of gut volume to body size makes the pony more efficient as a digester of plant fibre; and it may be this efficiency that makes it more likely to suffer from disorders such as laminitis and hyperlipaemia when it has access to food that is too rich. That these problems are especially common in the smallest of the ponies serves to confirm that they are directly linked to the diminutive size of these specimens of *Equus caballus* (the Latin name for the domestic horse/pony/cob).

At the other end of the equine forecourt, horses have their own set of problems that are specifically linked to being tall. For example, diseases like whistling and roaring, which involve a lack of control of the larynx, occur almost exclusively in horses and are particularly prevalent in exceptionally tall individuals. Because disorders of the respiratory tract are so common in really tall horses, the ceiling has more or less been reached in terms of breeding the biggest horse. Beyond 17.2 hands, wastage due to problems of this sort means that further breeding efforts are uneconomic.

Physical differences between horses and ponies rarely have repercussions when it comes to behaviour. Even when we take into consideration their smaller frames, ponies have particularly small heads, and especially tiny ears, when compared with horses, and to the human observer this has the effect of making a threatening grimace from a pony less dramatic than the equivalent from an aggressive Thoroughbred. Humans are generally not very good at reading equine body language. No doubt a horse would interpret such a gesture from a pony quite correctly, and perhaps this is why examples of domineering equine dwarfs are fairly thick on the ground.

My favourite has to be Seamus, who was the resident Shetland pony owned by the Australian ranch on which I used to work. At feeding time, all the working horses would be penned up individually and given their concentrate rations in recycled twenty-litre (5 gallon) metal containers. But the sides of the pens were not low enough to curb the advances of the little emperor, who would march from one pen to the next pillaging food from the occupants, who were often three times his size. As if to embellish his image, he would often have his head stuck in the feed tub from the previous pen as he moved to his next conquest – such was the intensity of his feeding frenzy. Images of Ned Kelly, the Australian outlaw famous for his taste in metallic millinery, would spring to mind.

Breed

The types of horse available to early man for domestication were products of natural selection and thus of the climate and terrain of the locality in which they evolved. It is from these original types that man has developed the different breeds. Thus the behaviour and conformation that we see in them are also products of the environmental conditions which moulded their ancestral types. Naturally, through artificial selection, man enhanced certain physical and behavioural characteristics which would increase a horse's

usefulness. These are called breed-dependent characteristics.

The ability to find shelter in response to the need for
it is a good example of a breed-dependent behaviour. As
representatives of a warm-blooded breed, Thoroughbreds
are more likely to stand still in cold weather and look miserable, while native ponies plump for the far more sensible
option of continuing their search for food or finding shelter.
Naturally, sheltering strategies involve a degree of learning
– as in the New Forest foal that follows its mother under
the cover of holly bushes when the rain sets in. However,
learning is just part of the story, since these animals' genes
have only survived by demanding that shelter be acquired.
The genes of Thoroughbreds, on the other hand, with their
more glamorous Persian origins, have not had to meet so
many challenging winters and so are less well attuned to the
advantages of shelter.

Similarly, in mountainous regions, the landscape has
favoured the selection of animals with innate sure-foot-
edness, and this comes with the ability to keep one's head
in a crisis – which is really another way of describing an
animal with a low reactivity score. Traditionally it is maintained that the Highland pony was developed for bringing
game down from the hills after a day's shooting. Clearly, a
horse that showed a tendency to tear off at speed every time
a grouse broke cover from underneath his feet would not
survive long in this tricky terrain.

Man can enhance Mother Nature's work by selecting
genes which influence behaviours that he favours. This
means more than simply selecting quieter horses, which are
predictably easier to ride. For instance, in parts of the world
where livestock are still mustered from the back of a horse,
the ability to pursue an errant herd member is an extremely
desirable equine behavioural trait. And it can be bred for,
along with the short back and low centre of gravity which
enhance a horse's ability to turn on the proverbial sixpence
and manoeuvre cattle back into or away from the herd. The
American Quarter-horse demonstrates these herding and
manoeuvring traits beautifully.

Another behaviour that is breed-specific is homing ability
which, while present in other breeds, is legendary in Icelandic ponies. Why the equines of a northern island should

Hungry carthorses have considerable pulling power.

have a refined talent for finding their way home is not clear. A similar characteristic is a feature of Herdwick sheep, who are adept at finding their way back to their birthplace. As a result, farmers with this ancient breed have to rely less on fencing to keep their stock in the locality. So perhaps this same ability has appealed through the centuries to Icelandic pony breeders. Indeed, the idea is by no means unattractive to me whenever I weigh up the merits of being able to ride back from the pub of an evening. Equally, having worked for a horse dealer as a child, I find the mischievous side of me speculating that this trait would be an excellent way of ensuring that you could sell the same horse many times over! Interestingly, the behaviour of Icelandic ponies is also breed-specific when it comes to gait, since they display the 'amble' which is somewhere between a walk and a trot.

The development of draught animals necessitated the selection of heavy creatures that could start to shift a wagon just by leaning into the collar. I have great affection for these characters, but I have to say that their ability to drag things along the ground is not confined to vehicles. Hungry carthorses have considerable pulling power, as anyone who has attempted to prevent a Shire mare from getting to her evening meal will testify. That lady is certainly not for turning! Heavier horses are not only the most awesome when it comes to barging but, similarly, they are notorious for leaning on the bit when being ridden. Also called 'working on the forehand', this offers another example of how breeding can influence behaviour.

The ways in which a horse's breed affects its behaviour can even involve body language, since the tools used for sending signals can differ from one breed to another. For instance, Arabian horses and their crosses are very demonstrative with their tails, rather like Pointer dogs are with their forepaws. An Arabian raises his tail with tremendous frequency but, most of the time, this is simply part of his way of balancing himself when moving. In contrast, the same elevation of the tail by a Dartmoor pony would indicate a display of amazement or exuberance.

Family group
Every time a horse owner decides to breed from an animal because of a particular physical or behavioural attribute, he is doing what horse breeders have done throughout the centuries. Any horse breeder will tell you that certain family groups display certain mental characteristics. This can influence the choice of stallion when the time comes to select a mating partner, for instance – a gentle stud will be favoured for use on a particularly talented but aggressive mare. Temperament is known to be under genetic influence, and it follows that behavioural problems like weaving and crib-biting have also been shown to arise in individual Thoroughbred families.

Naturally, we breed from horses which have performed successfully because we know that, quite apart from selecting for good physique, we have to select bloodlines which have the temperament to excel in particular disciplines. This sort of psychological feature can be as simple as the family's attitude to the type of work required. For example, the dams of top police horses are likely to have been more suited to crowd control than to winning the Two Thousand Guineas.

GENDER

It goes without saying that the males and females of a species perform certain behaviours to attract a mate and to ensure the survival of their genes. However, even out of the mating season, the behaviour of any animal is affected by its gender.

So, just as male dogs cock their legs while bitches tend to squat, so stallions and mares have different behavioural responses to the same stimulus. For example, when a stallion comes across a pile of manure he will go through a process of sniffing and maybe pawing but then will move over the pile before he himself defaecates or urinates. A mare may sniff at the dung, but if she leaves any message it will tend to be delivered in the spot where she is standing. This has interesting repercussions for pasture management. Because stallions create latrine areas that are so much more discrete than those of mares, they are more efficient at conservative grazing.

Other examples of the influence of gender on behaviour include greeting and vocalisation. The elevated prance of stallions and to a lesser extent geldings, when they encounter strange horses, has its origins in the ritualised displays used before mating. Equally, the trumpeting and grunting of a courting stallion are as gender-specific as the nickering of a nursing mare. The behaviour of a mare in spring and summer, far more than that of a stallion, is influenced by the changing levels of reproductive hormones in her body. Her responsiveness to stimuli and even her general mood are subject to cyclical flux, and this, along with the fact that most competition occurs at this time of year, helps to explain the preference we have for competing with male horses rather than females.

EXPERIENCE

When animals learn from one another, this is referred to as social learning. It occurs between mares and foals, since foals learn the bare necessities about grazing from their mothers. Foals that have been hand-reared are known to be less bold when exploring their environment, possibly because they have not been given the necessary cues by their mothers indicating that certain environments are safe enough to be investigated. Even in more normal circumstances, when weaning foals from their mothers we are asking them not only to consume foods other than milk but also to do without the comfort of their mothers, who have been their closest companions since birth. The behaviour of foals around the time of weaning speaks of considerable distress, unless affiliations with other youngsters or with an entire group of mares and foals can be established to give the foals some comfort.

The age of a horse has an effect on its attitude to stimuli, on the way early experience can be cross-referenced to similar stimuli in later life, and also to some extent on rank within a herd. This age effect is of importance when we train horses because we can capitalise on the fact that two- and three-year-olds are generally more curious than older horses and so are better able to learn from good experiences and strange sights and sounds. None the less, at any age a horse can learn from experiences – good or bad. The memory of horses is largely underestimated, a fact that should be borne in mind when we consider the effect that previous handling and training can have on their behaviour. The need for them to find themselves in positions of comfort and safety is also important here. For instance, if a horse has been asked to jump fences by a rider who tends to use the reins for balance, the horse will rapidly associate clearing a fence with receiving an acute jab of pain in the mouth. His strategy, not surprisingly, will be to approach the jumps with more caution and less enthusiasm. If the negative associations with jumping are continually reinforced the horse will eventually adopt refusal of the fence as his means of avoiding these repeated threats to his comfort and safety. As the rider kicks on to revive the dying pace, the horse associates the consequent flank discomfort with being around jumps in general, and he may go on to develop a completely stale attitude in the presence of coloured poles.

Examples of equine memory in laboratory tests are not well documented, but there are a few early studies in the academic literature which compare the memory of horses very favourably with that of elephants. We are told from an early age that elephants never forget, but this seems scarcely relevant because we are considerably more likely to find ourselves riding through the countryside on Beauty the Black than on Nellie the Elephant. My favourite tale of equine memory involves a pony called Pecos, who was taught to distinguish between twenty pairs of patterns in order to earn his carrot rewards. After a break of five months, he had retained more than 96 per cent of the information.

Since, as a vet student, I had to remember only 50 per cent of the information I had received in order to pass my end-of-year exams, I am in complete awe of Pecos!

MANAGEMENT

The modern riding horse has found himself in an environment quite different from that for which his ancestors evolved. The type of food he eats and his total food intake are controlled by his keeper, to suit the demands of his particular kind of work. Also, the bullying tactics of other horses may mean that he has to be protected when he tucks into his meals. Furthermore, in the winter months he may have his coat clipped so that he is less likely to sweat when he is asked to perform heavy exercise. As a consequence, he may need to be protected from cold and wet weather. And his owners may simply not have the time to brush caked mud off him before they take him out for a ride, so he is stabled.

Being stabled means that his movement is restricted. This is important for the trainers of racehorses because they have to be able to control daily exercise – the horses in their care need to have plenty of energy in reserve for training sessions, and so wandering around a field is regarded as an undesirable expenditure of energy. Consequently, like the majority of horses in work, they are required to be willing athletes on the one hand and contented prisoners on the other.

Restriction of movement is not the only price that horses have to pay when they are stabled. Their social life will also become limited if they have no neighbours. If they do have neighbours, these may not be the horses with whom they would choose to spend time if they were left to their own devices out in the field. Indeed, even if they are housed next door to their favourite companion, they cannot see him, smell him or touch him as much as they would be able to at grass.

We know from the increased number of respiratory diseases that horses get because of being stabled that the air quality in most loose-boxes is poor. It is worth remembering that, with their refined sense of smell, horses are probably far more aware of strong smells than are their owners. Horses are naturally coprophobic – in other words, they tend to avoid dung – but there are extended periods for any stabled horse when it simply cannot avoid its own dung. Indeed, it may have to lie down in it to roll or to rest.

The sights and sounds experienced by a stabled horse are certainly very different from those out in the paddock. The presence of walls means that he can see what is going on only by poking his head over the stable door. If sounds are emerging from somewhere outside his field of vision he is unable to get a clear understanding of what is going on. We do not know whether this frustrates him, but it certainly seems to change his response to sounds. In an attempt to gather as much information as possible about the world outside his loose-box, the horse will rush from his hay net to the door whenever he hears hoofbeats, neighs or the arrival of food. Therefore, the reason why horses spend extended periods loafing over their stable doors may be linked to both a desire to avoid unpleasant smells and to the need to gather information.

Since horses have evolved to respond to changes in the length of daylight in ways which maximise the chances of reproducing successfully, lighting can affect hormonal balance. Mares do not come into season during the winter because eleven months later their foals would be born into a world which was particularly cold. Keeping warm in the cold season is not impossible, but it requires food for energy. And when one is born without a full set of teeth this food has to come from Mum, who has to graze to provide the energy for milk production. This is where the main problem lies, because in the winter months the grass is not growing and is thus a very poor source of nutrition. So it makes very good sense to exercise some rudimentary family planning and to breed only when one has the resources to support one's offspring to the stage of weaning.

When we race young Thoroughbreds, we group them according to the year of their birth. So we attempt to breed foals earlier in the year because they will have a better chance when raced against their peers born in the summer months. To do this we use artificial lighting in the mares' stables, to add to the day length and thus persuade them to come into season as they would do in the spring. The danger is that the more we understand about the physiology of our horses, the more likely we are to be tempted to alter their behaviour further by confinement and artificial manipulations. Each time we move horses further from their natural state, we invite behavioural abnormalities as well as threatening their natural reproductive fitness.

Diet

When we stable horses the food we offer them is in a defined spot, the hay is in a hay net and the concentrated feed in a feed bowl or manger. It may at first seem particularly benevolent of us to help horses out by not asking them to work to find their food. The stabled horse cannot know that he is the product of a process called evolution, nor does he know that this process designed him to be an animal that walked around for sixteen hours a day while nourishing itself. However, it is possible that animals have in-built needs to perform certain behaviours for the sake of performing them, rather than because they achieve a specific goal. In the same way we have to have hobbies, even though they do not appear to affect our health nor do they earn us a living. By housing horses we have eliminated the possibility for them to perform the wandering search, one of the most important features of their grazing behaviour.

In the feral state horses rarely have the inclination or the opportunity to eat dried feedstuffs. In a drought, dried-out pasture will have lost much of its nutritional value because it is no longer growing, and reserves of energy will have been sent down to the root system. All the same, as the summer months wear on horses will pick away at the seed-heads of grasses, and this is essentially why they are able to digest the cereals that we tend to feed them as a concentrated source of nourishment. It is largely because hay and cereals are in a semi-preserved state and are easier to store and handle than their fresh counterparts that we use them to feed housed herbivores such as cattle and horses. However, the fact that these foods are not bulked out with their original water content means that the animals take in large amounts of nutrient very rapidly, and we have to consider this when we take them off the pasture and start to feed them hay and cereals. It has been said many times that the digestive system of horses was not designed by a plumber – the numerous U-bends and junctions can cope with a diet of succulent grass very efficiently, but the introduction of harder foods brings with it the risk of blockages and episodes of rapid fermentation which can upset the fine balance of the digestive process.

Continual access to clean drinking water is certainly one of the bonuses of domestic life. In the feral state, trips to a water source are as frequent as the climate and the water content of the foodstuffs demand. The same is true in a stable, and some horses even learn that eating hay is easier if most mouthfuls are dunked in water before being chewed.

We know that after their evening meal thirteen million Britons happily occupy themselves with another episode of *Coronation Street*. But horses, in the absence of any fascination for the latest gossip from the Rover's Return and with concentrated foods requiring little chewing, are often left with time on their hands, so to speak. In fact, of course, horses may have a quite different appreciation of time from ours, but what cannot be disputed is that the equine mouth, the machinery that has evolved to munch away for 70 per cent of a grazing horse's day, is now required to lie idle between feeds, as are the legs that were designed to carry the animal from one patch of grass to the next. Since horses are not robots they cannot simply switch off their machinery, so during such times of temporary redundancy there is a rise in their motivation to perform these natural behaviours. And where this motivation cannot be satisfied, unnatural replacement behaviours develop.

It would make sense for an animal that spends so much of its day foraging to be selective when doing so. Survival can depend on acquiring good-quality sources of energy through feeding, and the grazing behaviour of horses is indeed a search for the leafier grass plants rather than the older stems. It appears that the calorific value of foodstuffs can influence horses' choice – a fact that the manufacturers of horsefeed have used in order to make their products more palatable. For example, treacle (or molasses) has an instant appeal because it is laden with calories, and mint flavouring is attractive to horses because it is associated with very sugary sweets. Furthermore, the palatability of food can affect behaviour in curious ways. For instance, in horses which repetitively crib-bite (an abnormal mouthing behaviour seen mostly in stabled horses), a more palatable meal causes an increase in intensity of the behaviour. Current research in the United States aims to establish why this should be.

Another feature of domestic horse nutrition that can affect behaviour is the timing of feeds. Fortunately for us, rhythms in a horse's natural feeding behaviour mean that more food is consumed during daylight hours than at night. This fits in with our desire to delivery concentrate food to our stabled horses at what we would consider to be a sociable hour. However, horses are naturally trickle feeders – they consume little and often – and the bucket of cereal that a horse in heavy work receives is a far cry from what he would call a trickle. In fact, being fed a bucketful of concentrates is the equine equivalent of hitting the jackpot, while hay represents the routine pay-packet. This analogy gives us an insight into why horses' behaviour can change so much as far as food is concerned; the excitement that is generated by the promise of a daily jackpot win is considerable, and frustration arises when the promised bonanza is not delivered instantly. This explains why so many owners tell me that their horse weaves his head from side to side only before being fed. The level of anticipation created by the rattling of a feed bucket is recognised by anyone who uses this auditory cue to attract horses in a field.

Horses must have a different experience of appetite from our own. Whereas their stomachs were developed to be almost continually topped up, we humans, as hunters and gatherers, had the capacity to gorge ourselves when a plentiful food source was encountered. So we are probably better designed to go without food than the horses in our stables. In the feral state, grazing is interrupted by sleep only for one or two hours at a time, but the domesticated animal often finishes his hay net around midnight and then has to wait another five or six hours before having something called 'breakfast'.

As well as controlling the quality, quantity and frequency of the food offered to our stabled horses, we also control its vitamin and mineral content. The importance of 'micronutrients' should not be overlooked, since horses seem to know better than we do when they are experiencing a deficiency and will work to acquire them. I am convinced that this is why groups of horses can be found grinding their way through mouthfuls of mud while surrounded by lush grazing. Given anecdotal reports of such curious cravings, we should be very cautious about our definition of pica, or depraved appetite, in the horse.

Similarly, we must bear in mind that horses, more than most animals, have a need for roughage in their diets. To deny them access to sufficient plant fibre is often a catalyst for wood-chewing which, sadly, is regarded by many owners as a 'stable vice'. To attach the label 'vice' to a behaviour is to imply that the animal is in some way responsible and that he is performing it with vicious intent. A more scientific approach to this eating anomaly would be to accept that our understanding of the nutrition of horses is by no means complete. For example, traditional horsefolk will give their charges access to coal and gorse without claiming to know what benefit they may offer or why, from time to time, they should be eaten with such gusto. Equally, we know that oats have a 'heating', or over-exciting, effect on the behaviour of ponies and, to some degree, horses. Some equine nutritionists account for this phenomenon by reminding us that chocolate can have similar effects on certain small children, to the extent that it can make them behave as though they have recently consumed hard drugs! Beyond that we do not know what it is about oats that elicits this change in behaviour, nor do we know why ponies are generally so much more sensitive to their effect.

Exercise

Food intake can certainly affect a horse's inclination and ability to perform heavy work. Like most quadrupeds, the horse carries his stomach in close proximity to his diaphragm, against which lie his lungs. The presence of a full cargo of 15 litres ($16^1/_2$ quarts) of roughage tends to reduce the efficiency with which the lungs expand and contract – which is why we tend to reduce food intake before exercise and why we should avoid feeding fatigued horses until their respiratory rate has returned to normal.

The significance of exercise differs as between man and horse. For example, a horse's desire to run may originate in play but, more importantly, the ability to run comes from the need to escape from predators. We, meanwhile, exercise horses for the leisure and competitive appeal that horse-riding holds. It seems likely, therefore, that the gradual introduction of work at different paces, for the sake of ensuring musculoskeletal fitness before exertion, must be very difficult for horses to understand. They cannot know that six weeks of exercise at a relatively slow pace is the recommended way of avoiding tendon damage. This regime seems to be especially frustrating for horses that have become accustomed to galloping in particular parts of their locality. After a period of rest, daily outings during the lengthy fittening process have to avoid areas that have strong associations with reckless displays of speed.

For health reasons, horsefolk are careful to give their charges regular daily exercise and they ensure that days off are accompanied by a cut in energy intake. This approach has tremendous merit, in that it evokes a sense of routine which allows the horse to adjust its stable behaviour in anticipation of imminent ridden work. This is why experienced hunters refuse their breakfast on the mornings of a meet – having learned to associate procedures like being plaited up with the promise of fast work in equine company, they become too excited to stand quietly and feed.

It pays to consider the effect that the amount of exercise can have on a horse's attitude to work and on his general behaviour. From our own experience, we know that a feeling of fatigue can be accompanied by exhilaration. This does not come from a sense of achievement alone, because we can get a buzz from running twenty-six miles without actually winning the London Marathon. In the short term extended periods of work can lead to exhaustion, with the horse having to rest before resuming the business of eating. Once he becomes fitter and more accustomed to heavy work, these rest periods become shorter and his thirst for exercise can become difficult to meet. Like humans who experience the 'jogger's high', it is possible that equine athletes generate their own natural pain-killers, called endorphins. If these bring with them a sense of well-being, the horse may learn that to keep producing them is rewarding. This may be why I am often told of endurance horses that will spend all night box-walking, or in some cases box-trotting, after a forty-mile race.

The use of the whip can undoubtedly affect behaviour and is a particularly contentious welfare issue of long standing. As with any form of punishment, or negative reinforcement, one has to be extremely careful about when in a given set of circumstances one applies the pain. How many times do we see horses refuse a jump by charging off to one side of the obstacle or the other? This is usually followed by a short struggle before the rider pulls the horse up to a more controlled pace and then gives it a belting. It is worth considering whether that horse has associated the pain with the refusal to jump, or with the fact that he was eventually pulled up. Horses have such good memories that there is a place for the light use of a whip as a reinforcer when the animal has not responded to a more subtle signal. In fact, even carrying a whip without ever actually using it can also change his behaviour.

In discussing different horse types, I mentioned that 'warm-bloods' tend to be more flighty, or reactive. This means that when being trained they may respond to more subtle stimuli than their thicker-skinned 'cold-blooded' classmates. This responsiveness can be preserved by only ever applying delicate pressure with the legs and hands. Conversely, the heavy-handed approach to equitation effectively leads to a numbing of the gums where the bit lies and the horse is said to have become 'hard-mouthed'. The tendency of riding-school horses to be unresponsive has similar origins, in that these are the paragons of patience who have to put up with novice riders constantly giving contradictory leg and hand signals. The rider's flapping legs say 'Go', while the reins, rather selfishly pulled to assist his or her balance, are saying 'Stop'. So unresponsiveness prevails, and as the years of a school horse's life go by, instructors tend to find themselves using the words 'Kick him' far more often than 'Praise him'.

I am often asked if horses know when they have won a race or a show-jumping class, and it is a source of considerable annoyance to some people when I explain that it is not possible. To know one has won, one has to know in the first place that one has been competing. If we stop to consider what competition means to horses, we remember that they have evolved to compete for resources, such as food and water. Winning these natural prizes rarely involves racing one another or jumping fences, so these activities are irrelevant to natural forms of equine competition. Horses cannot know that it is essential to be in the lead at the point on the Aintree race-course where the crowds are gathered (the finishing post). At Hickstead they cannot know that the previous horse's clear round means that they have to do the same in a faster time in order to earn applause. However, what *is* likely is that owners and riders can transmit a sense of elation, which the horse may learn to associate with praises and rewards. This can enhance performance, but not competitiveness.

Regardless of whether our horses are competing or working to earn their crust, the work clothes that we make them wear can have a resounding impact on their behaviour. All over the world people use a variety of saddles, bridles and bits on their horses, ponies and donkeys. The extent to which these pieces of saddlery actually fit the wearers without causing discomfort or pain has not been assessed, but we do know that even if a saddle is expertly fitted it will probably fit less well the moment the animal loses or gains weight. The times we have to adjust a rucksack during a morning's walk should give us some idea of the pressures that come to bear when we put tack on our horses. We know that back pain of this sort can be sufficient to put them off jumping as readily as can bad riding. So it is not unreasonable to imagine that riding on the flat is also affected, and that a horse's general behaviour when ridden will suffer. In the same way we can alter the behaviour and responsiveness of a horse by introducing a different bit: in most instances, we tend to reach for a 'stronger' bit when we are experiencing problems of control. In fact, what we are resorting to is simply a more painful device, or one that applies an equivalent pain to a different part of the head.

Finally, on occasions when we withdraw exercise, we always have to bear in mind the considerable psychological challenge that this can represent to fit horses. They may spend one day cavorting across the countryside in the company of other horses, ridden by people in bright red jackets, and the next day be turned out into a paddock with a geriatric grey mare with a very furry coat. A far worse warning of imminent boredom comes when the veterinary surgeon, having watched the horse trot up the lane, utters the words, 'Six weeks' box rest'. This probably makes the notion of day after day in the field with the old dear in grey seem like paradise. Box rest can seldom be what it is intended to be, since the horse can still wander around his 'hospital ward' and can do so at the trot if he feels like it. Equally, the first trot after a period of enforced rest so regularly turns into a leap, a lurch and a canter that one is left wondering whether any putative healing process has been undone.

CURRENT CONDITIONS

Given that long-term factors like genetics, past experience, diet and confinement can affect behaviour, it makes sense to consider the influence of shorter-term conditions such as the effect of companions and their behaviour.

When one animal's behaviour prompts the same behaviour in another we describe it as *social facilitation*. This feature of horse behaviour has its origins in the fact that horses have evolved to live in herds. Graphic examples include mass visits to watering-holes which are often initiated by an individual herd member, and the escape manoeuvres demonstrated by a group of ponies when only one of them has actually perceived a possible danger. The extent to which a ridden horse can be controlled in galloping equine company is related to the need that he has to behave in response to his peers.

Even the season of the year can have an influence on a horse's behaviour, in that prevailing weather conditions seem to affect the way he or she feels. For example, some horses abhor getting wet. These are the ones who seem to try to curl themselves into a ball while being ridden in driving rain but only succeed in pulling the most miserable of faces, with ears pinned back and lips pursed. Then there are those who find windy days particularly stimulating – stimulating in the purest sense of the word, since the rapid passage of air sends a cascade of smells into their nostrils while flying leaves and debris provide rushes of movement and noise. Thus horses' tendency to spook at things unseen by their riders seems to peak in the leafy days of autumn. Winter then brings a deal of muddy rides and sometimes days with no exercise at all which, for the stabled horse, must be a source of considerable frustration. When the ice that has kept him in his stable has melted, the first outing is always the time when he displays more *joie de vivre* than anyone has bargained for.

So, the *complete* answer to the question, 'What affects a horse's behaviour?', has to include 'almost everything in its genetic make-up, its past experience and its current environment'.

Part Two

WHAT IS A HORSE?

3

WILD HORSE—FERAL HORSE— DOMESTIC HORSE

The question 'Why does my horse . . .?' is very often answered with 'Because it is a horse'. In other words, much of what we regard as problem behaviour can be explained in terms of normal horse behaviour, as I have indicated in Chapter 1. Having touched on the myriad factors that can influence the way a horse behaves, I shall now consider the many features of normal horse behaviour that account for what we see in paddocks and stables every day. The first in this series, '*Why Does My Dog . . .?*, expanded our understanding of canine behaviour by cross-referencing to the behaviour patterns in wolves that have been studied in a truly wild state. Unfortunately, the same facility does not exist for students of equine behaviour since the only truly wild equine species is the zebra, which does not bear close comparison since it has a radically different number of chromosomes from the domestic horse.

The Mongolian wild horse, or Przewalski's horse, became extinct in the wild in the 1950s, perhaps because so few could agree on how to pronounce its name! Fortunately, the current population is buoyant and reintroduction programmes are under way in France and the Ukraine. However, so far as being suitable as research material is concerned, these horses must be regarded with extreme caution since many purists insist that any population which has lived in captivity for more than two generations can be considered domesticated. Much as I would like to see these purists attempt something as straightforward as a quiet hack on one of these 'domesticated' beasties, I take their point. So we are left with one family of *Equus* to turn to in our quest for wild horse behaviour – feral horses. These are the descendants of domestic horses and ponies that fell out of the clutches of enforced husbandry many generations ago by being abandoned, released or, in some cases, even ship-wrecked. The appeal of these horses for hippophiles lies in their regression to type. That is, as the constraints of living in the wild have come to bear on successive generations of feral horse, many of the anatomical and behavioural traits that were selected by man have disappeared. What remains, therefore, offers the possibility of a useful estimation of the sort of animal that man began to domesticate more than five thousand years ago.

A TO Z OF NORMAL HORSE BEHAVIOUR

The pages that follow attempt to highlight the intriguing features of feral horse behaviour and relate them to dom-estic equivalents. Much of what I have included will bring a knowing smile to your face when you think of some of your own experiences around horses. Beyond the familiar, I have tried to bring in as much up-to-date research as possible as well as the occasional sprinkling of controversy and con-jecture.

A. Aggression
Aggression and threats are the horse's way of protecting itself, its offspring, and its resources. Behavioural scientists give the whole gamut of disputes, threats and combat that are shown by a species the title *agonistic behaviour.*

Agonistic displays such as the ear-pinning, nose-wrinkling and kick threats that horses use are of tremendous value to social animals because they help to avoid combat. They give animals the chance to settle their differences without coming to blows. If threats were not an option, every dispute would end in a physical confrontation with the accompany-ing exhaustion and injuries that, in themselves, have the potential to compromise fitness and jeopardise the survival of both the winner and the loser.

Play-fighting is an important rehearsal for the tussles that arise in later life, but intriguingly it is restricted to male foals. If a colt tries this sort of game with a filly she will soon send him packing with glares, bites and kicks. This may be because the manoeuvres used in inter-male combat are quite different from those that a pair of squabbling mares tends to deploy. Mares that have decided to fight after a head-to-head exchange of snorts and curses usually turn round and back into each other, squealing and kicking. It is usual for them then to lean into one another quite heavily. Submission at this point marks the end of the exchange, because the first mare to back off has to move away quickly as this is the point at which she is most likely to be kicked.

When males fight, on the other hand, they do so face to face. They start by striking out at each other but, as the dispute escalates, the exchange develops to include rearing and biting. In this form of head-on combat, a stallion is aiming to rise to his maximum height while biting his opponent's mouth. Mouth-biting during these preliminaries is capable of knocking an opponent completely off balance. Once on the ground a fighting horse is at his most vulnerable, because maximum damage can be inflicted upon him while he is least able to defend himself.

Gender is not the only factor to influence the type of agonistic behaviour that is seen in equine communities. For example, aggression can fluctuate with the time of year. Stallions are more likely to fight among themselves when mares in season are around. The breeding season is the same cue for aggression in Przewalski's mares, who direct their attention to other females in an attempt to keep the stallion for themselves. Agonistic behaviours between members of the opposite sex increase during periods when mating is possible, because they can keep stallions at bay until the mare is at her most fertile. Furthermore, aggression can become self-directed in breeding stallions that are denied access to a mate. The incidence of flank-biting is greatest in housed stallions during the breeding season and can be treated far more successfully by liberation than by sedation.

It may surprise some horse owners to learn that, once they are established, feral horse communities are more peaceful than domestic horse groups. This is because groups that form in the wild are stable, whereas in domesticity there is a constant flux as horses are removed from and returned to the group – for instance, to be ridden or to be housed overnight. This instability means that rank has to be checked and re-established regularly, giving rise to twenty times more

agonistic displays in domestic than in feral horse populations. In addition, domestic situations have the added
hazard of fencing, which is the undoing of many subordinate horses because it prevents their escaping from the
aggressive advances of dominant field-mates. The most
common cause of dispute between domestic horses is, of
course, food. Those confined to paddocks are often rather
crowded in comparison with their feral cousins foraging on
extensive plains. Understandably, they jealously guard their
bucket of feed or pile of hay. It's all part of the 'survival of
the fittest', food being a major contribution to fitness.

While horses instinctively flee, when captured or cornered
they will fight. This defensive form of combat is seen also
in mares that protect their foals against strangers,
especially in the first month of life. Nursing mothers can
also be quite violent to alien foals in order to preserve milk
supplies for their own youngster who has yet to learn how
to protect his own resources. Learning plays a vital role in
the development of agonistic behaviour in juvenile horses,
because foals must learn how to hold their own in equine
company without breaking any social taboos. The importance of socialisation for youngstock is evident to anyone
who has compared foals that have been reared in isolation
with those that have been group-reared. The lack of social
graces in isolated youngsters arises because they have never
learned to define the borders between play and aggression.

Horses in captivity can learn to be unnaturally aggressive,
and this is discussed in Part Three.

B. Bachelor groups
When they reach sexual maturity in the wild, juvenile male
horses tend to disperse from the group into which they were
born because of pressure from the harem stallion. Where
these homeless youths end up is highly dependent on circumstance, with some finding mixed-sex groups of the same
age and others remaining solitary for prolonged periods.
The most usual eventuality is that colts aggregate to form
bachelor groups. Despite being bound by only transient
affiliations, members of these herds have been known to
react aggressively to the appearance of strangers in the same
way that harem stallions do. We do not yet understand the
criteria for admission to the bachelor 'gang'.

Stallions that lose their harems to superior males are ejected from the vicinity of their home range and find themselves isolated from social groupings unless they are fortunate enough to come across a stray female. Alternatively, they too may join a transient bachelor band which will allow them to reap the benefits of living in an equine group. Here the ejected stallion will consort with young males who make up the bulk of the group. Together, deposed stallions and weaned colts can groom each other and play-fight. This prepares and maintains their ability to struggle for harem ownership and mating rights. In this way, the bachelor herd can be viewed as a management training camp for prospective equine executives! The usual group size of two or three members occasionally rises beyond eight, but then becomes unstable and liable to split up.

Understanding how horses organise themselves socially in the wild helps humans to maintain harmony in domesticated groups. Large yards, with occupants continually coming and going, encounter least aggression when they keep males and females apart. The geldings form a bachelor group, while the mares behave as they would in a bonded stallionless harem.

C. Communication

Horses communicate by using their sense of sight, hearing, smell and taste. Sometimes the message is a simple 'I was here.' But we believe that they can also communicate such elaborate concepts as a stallion's ownership of a receptive female.

Sight

Displays from one horse to another chiefly involve the head, neck and tail, which are the most mobile parts of their bodies. For example, the position of the ears indicates to the observer, human or equine, the direction of the sounds a horse is listening to. Horses are expert at communicating via body language – so skilled, in fact, that they can read *our* body postures. Two obvious signals that even we humans can understand are aggressive ear-flattening and the raising of the tail before moving off.

Visual stimuli are also used by horses to indicate their presence. Marks like rolling sites, rubbing spots and the unmissable piles of faeces left by stallions are tell-tale clues that horses have been around. These are apparent to any human observer, so they must be considerably more intriguing and informative to any exploring horse that encounters them. (*See also* Vision, p. 69).

Hearing
The characteristic rhythm of hoofbeats, especially at the trot, will evoke a response in most listening horses. It is a sound which usually excites other horses that are some distance away to vocalise and move towards the source of the sound. To signal different needs and intentions, horses use their vocal cords to generate a number of different sounds. For example, in reproductive interactions sounds can range from the gentle nickers that a stallion uses in courtship to announce his intention to copulate to the squeals that an unreceptive mare emits to reject his suggestions.

It is important to remember that our understanding of animals' auditory sense is very much in its infancy. For instance, the way in which equine sounds are organised in relation to each other has not been studied in depth, and it may be that the meaning of one noise differs radically when followed or preceded by another.

Taste and smell
Horses have senses of taste and smell that are delicately interwoven. For instance, when a mare delivers a foal, she licks its coat partly as an attempt to dry it off, but also as a means of identifying its characteristic flavour and scent for future reference. The information she gathers at the birth serves as a benchmark that she can use to confirm thereafter that the foal nuzzling her for nourishment is her own. It is not long before she can perform this ID check by sniffing alone.

The mobility of horses' nostrils tells us a great deal about the role that smell plays in their lives. For instance, when they have their heads down to graze they still flex and flare their nostrils. This gives them a steady stream of information about the grazing that lies ahead, including to what extent it is contaminated with faecal material. The accuracy of this sense is demonstrated by stabled horses, which are so incredibly adept at sorting nourishing strands of hay from their less wholesome beds. This reliance on smell when eating also explains in part the loss of appetite we see when they have nasal discharges.

For further examples of olfactory communication, we have only to observe the way horses exchange odours when they meet one another for the first time, or after a period of separation. They start by sniffing each other's breaths and then move on to inspect the whole body. The sniffer thereby learns a great deal, including what the other horse has been eating and its state of health. The scent given off by skin is a cocktail that includes sweat from recent exercise and sebum secreted to lubricate hair shafts. Although horses are clearly fascinated by all these odours, we cannot be sure how they interpret the information that they impart. The smell of skin is also thought to communicate information about current diet, and even kinship. Similarly, the groin is an important centre for odours and for pheromones that signify gender and reproductive status. All of these factors account for the interest horses take in sniffing sites all over the body when they meet. (*See also* Olfaction, p. 59; Taste, p. 67.)

D. Drinking

Drinking bouts vary in frequency depending on the ambient temperature, the availability of water and lactation status, while the volume of water intake is also linked to bodyweight and even breed. The 'typical' horse is said to spend about fifteen minutes a day drinking and to consume about 36 litres (9-10 gallons) each day.

Horses drink by immersing their lips below the surface of the water and drawing it in with a sucking action, while swallowing approximately once a second. During a single bout, over four litres (one gallon) can be consumed before the horse takes a break to have a look around. In free-ranging situations, the accessibility of watering-holes has an effect on the number of visits made each day: when water is a considerable distance from grazing sites, herds will make only one visit, but when it is readily available they drink small amounts several times a day. Army horses can therefore be watered as a group on a regimented schedule of visits to a water trough three times a day instead of being provided with a bucket of water per stall. But the fact that this is possible does not necessarily make it desirable, since it reduces the choice that individual animals can make. Restricted freedom of choice may engender frustration, which is associated with poor welfare.

In the feral context, the more dominant members of a group drink first. This means that in drought conditions subordinate individuals risk having to drink cloudy dregs or, worse still, nothing at all. Separate bands of horses take turns to visit watering-holes in order to avoid the mixing of mares, which the various harem stallions would then have to sort out with energy-consuming disputes.

Feral horses are often reluctant to drink when they are rounded up. This is because the smell of a familiar water source is a prerequisite for horses to be able to relax when drinking. Anyone who has encouraged horses to drink at a show will recognise this apparent fussiness, and this is why many competitors take their own water to events. Reluctance to drink is also a considerable problem when water sources are contaminated or aversive for other reasons, such as stray electricity from automatic waterers. Some horses can be so sensitive as to go off their water when moved from one site to another. The introduction of water from the old yard is effective but hardly practical, so before the move most owners add a flavouring such as a few drops of peppermint essence, which can easily be continued afterwards. If preventive or remedial steps are not taken, reluctance to drink can even lead to clinical dehydration and impactions of the bowel. Thus, for stabled horses, buckets are the favoured means of providing water – they can be cleaned easily and the consumption level can be monitored.

Urine output is not directly related to water consumption since so many other factors can affect the destination of water that a horse drinks. In fact, of the many litres (quarts) that it consumes in a day less than a quarter is passed as urine. This is because most of a horse's water loss occurs through the airways, the bowels and the skin in breath, faeces and sweat, respectively.

E. Eating
From their first day of life, foals often nibble at blades of grass. They are, however, better designed for milk-drinking than for grazing, since they have only rudimentary teeth

and their legs are so long in proportion to their necks that they have to splay them out to reach the ground.

Grazing is the usual means of ingestion in the adult, but browsing is also adopted, particularly when grass becomes scarce. Although legumes and grasses are preferred to shrubs and herbs, there is apparently no correlation between the energy content of a given species of forage and the amount voluntarily consumed. While preferred grasses have variable fibre and soluble carbohydrate contents, they are juicier and less salty than non-preferred forages. So it seems that taste is the key sense used to select favoured forages, and this sense is also used to some extent to avoid toxic plants with low palatability. Smell too plays a significant role in diet selection, and particularly in the way horses avoid areas contaminated with equine faeces. Other factors that influence the way they select their feed include its relative hardness, as indicated by their adeptness at rejecting clumps of soil that enter their mouths via the roots of plants. This fussiness allows horses to graze more safely than, say, cattle, which are notorious for consuming foreign bodies and thereby precipitating abdominal catastrophes. Thankfully, the veterinary literature very rarely makes any reference to colic in horses that have made unwise selections when dining.

Horses spend an average of ten to twelve hours a day grazing, but when forage is scarce the grazing period may exceed nineteen hours. Peaks in foraging occur in the early morning and late afternoon, with bouts lasting from thirty minutes to four hours. Time allocations for feral horses are similar to those of domestic horses at grass, with a similar diurnal rhythm of foraging. Horses' meal-times are not confined to daylight hours: grazing is also a common activity at night, often accounting for more than 50 per cent of all recorded behaviour.

Essentially, eating in horses is an opportunistic behaviour, since it can be manipulated to capitalise on the type of forage accessible within a given terrain. Although grass is the main source of nutrition, this may simply be because it is so readily available. In habitats where other vegetation predominates, horses forage on buds, bark, leaves, fruit, submerged aquatic plants and even seaweed.

F. Foaling and foals

A number of anatomical changes are found in the normal mare before she gives birth. These changes – such as the accumulation of a waxy secretion on the ends of the teats – signify her preparation for the passage of a foal through the pelvic canal and the subsequent production of milk. At the same time as her body is adjusting before giving birth, the mare's behaviour also changes. In a bid to be left alone, she may begin to drift away from her companions. This search for isolation, however, is not seen in all mares, and it is thought to be related to their age and rank, with older and higher-ranking females travelling up to five kilometres (three miles) from the natal band. It is not clear why subordinate band members do not follow dominant wanderers at this stage, as one might expect. Perhaps a subtle form of signalling that breaks down social facilitation (see p. 213) will one day be detected in mares as they approach labour.

The selection of suitable terrain for the birth is significant for some mares that use sloping ground to assist the passage of their foal. However, for most mares, the absence of distraction seems to be the most important factor. The control they can impose on the time of their foaling is considerable, and domestic mares are very good at expelling their offspring the moment that their owners' self-imposed vigil is interrupted. In the wild, this is important because mares giving birth are vulnerable to attack from predators. The rapidity and secrecy of birth explain why normal foalings are so rarely witnessed by humans and tend to occur at night. Some observers suggest that humans' need for lights during equine parturition is what mares finds most aversive about their interference.

The actual business of foaling is heralded by sweating, flank-watching, rolling and circling, all of which speak to horsefolk of abdominal pain. This restless period may last for a matter of minutes or for hours, and marks the first stage of labour. The second stage begins with the appearance of the foetal sac and the subsequent 'breaking of the waters'. As the mare lies down to deal with her major contractions, further volumes of amniotic fluid are usually passed. Although she may stand up and then lie down again several times during this stage of labour, she is usually on her side when the foal emerges. The contraction process is certainly very rapid once the torpedo-shaped infant has been lined up for expulsion. In fact, the average length of the second stage is less than twenty minutes. The third stage, the passing of the placenta, occurs an hour or so later.

Being present when one's own mare gives birth is a privilege bestowed on few owners, and it is certainly not one that should be abused by the offer of over-enthusiastic assistance. Research on Thoroughbred studs in Newmarket has highlighted the importance of restraint on the part of human observers when attending equine births. For instance, they should not encourage mares to get to their feet too readily once their foals are born, because this can prematurely stop the passing of valuable placental blood reserves to the foal through the umbilical cord. Such a loss of blood brings down oxygen levels in the foal's brain to dangerously low levels, and can expose the youngster to the risk of brain damage. The relatively low incidence of foaling problems and brain-damaged foals in feral horse populations seems to indicate that the over-zealous human interference seen in domestic contexts has the potential to compromise trouble-free foalings and the health of foals.

The development of behaviours in the new-born foal has been catalogued many times by serious foal-watchers and cannot be dealt with fully in this volume. We all know that human mothers are keen to log the development of milestone behaviours such as smiling, crawling, talking and walking in their babies. The same is true of breeders, who by monitoring behavioural achievements can be reassured that their foals are developing normally. Compared with human development, the emergence of different behaviours in the repertoire of a foal follows a rapid sequence. For example, when only half an hour old the typical foal is able to focus, and within an hour it is expected to be able to follow and suckle its dam. It also struggles when restrained. After two hours it has learned to recognise its dam and can readily vocalise in order to find her and seek shelter at her side. Other behaviours such as trotting, galloping, rolling, scratching, rubbing and flehmen (see p. 138) have all been recorded in foals within twenty-four hours of birth.

The early resistance of foals to human restraint has been studied closely by some American researchers, who feel that it can be overcome at this early stage to improve their tractability in later life. These most interesting imprinting studies have prompted the introduction of human mannequins to the foaling boxes of some studs.

G. Gaits

On open ranges, horses have been shown to travel up to 80 km (50 miles) daily – for example, to visit their water-hole. For pastured horses grazing is the main initiator of locomotion, and resources are usually more concentrated than in feral contexts. The distance travelled per day depends less on the location of water than simply the availability of food and the time that is devoted to foraging. Even in a field, the distance travelled each day by domestic horses at pasture has been estimated at 20 km (12 miles). Locomotion is also used in communication and courtship, and since the horse is essentially a creature of flight it is vital as its main anti-predator strategy. Furthermore, movement plays a considerable role in equine recreation, with up to three-quarters of the kinetic activity of foals being in the form of play.

Given that movement and locomotion form such an important part of horse behaviour, it is not surprising that their gaits have been the subject of many anatomical studies. Some veterinary experts recognise twelve different gaits, but many of these have been selected for artificially or taught to the horse. Natural equine gaits can be whittled down to three types: the walk, the trot and the gallop, all of which employ different rhythms and sequences of footfalls. Most importantly, these gaits offer horses different speeds that lie in the range of approximately seven, ten and thirty kilometres (four, six and eighteen miles) per hour, respectively.

The gaits of a horse are very much like the gears of a car: there is an appropriate ratio of energy to speed for any given type of terrain or situation. The walk is the most common gait, since it is the one used in grazing. Grazing at the trot is not effective, although some trekking ponies are capable of roadside snacks at any pace! Depending on the quality of the pasture and its hunger, a typical horse will take between two and five mouthfuls of grass for every footstep. The prevalence of walking can also be explained by virtue of the fact that it is the most economical pace and that it can be tailored to the horse's state of fatigue. For example, in a normal walk stride the hindfeet tend to overtake the impression left by the forefeet whereas in a tired stride they tend to lag, a measure that riding instructors, for instance, use to estimate the willingness of a horse to work – many stale school horses tend to offer the most uninterested shuffle when given the choice.

The trot is the two-beat action used as a sustainable gait when horses are removing themselves from potential danger; it is interspersed with walking if considerable distances have to be covered. The gallop is reserved for short bouts of play and, perhaps more importantly, for real emergencies to avoid a would-be predator or when a horse has been cornered by an angry and higher-ranking herd member.

H. Herds and harems

Being a member of a herd offers tremendous advantages to an animal that is obliged to spend most of its day foraging. When a horse's head is down its view of any advancing threat, particularly from behind, is limited. When it is in a group with other horses it can continue to graze in the knowledge that there are so many more pairs of eyes and ears on the look-out for trouble. But watch any horse eating and drinking and you'll soon notice that its head is not always at ground level. It raises it at intervals to take in information from all around, and this vigilance is useful not only in detecting early alarm signals in fellow horses but also in checking for signs that they have come across a particularly tasty patch of herbage.

The elements of teamwork are also evident in herds of horses at rest. A horse spends only a small percentage of its time resting on the ground, as when it does so it is placing itself at some risk of predation because its getaway in the event of attack will be slower than it would be from a standing start. And it is very rare to see an entire group resting on the ground at the same time. The role of vigilante rotates so that every adult member takes a turn. The same turn-taking process applies with rolling, since this is the equine equivalent of being caught with one's pants down and leaves the exposed animal vulnerable to predation. It is therefore a mark of trust when a horse will roll in the presence of humans.

The disadvantage of being in a group is that each individual is in direct competition with its herd-mates for resources. It has been suggested that herd animals exist in groups only because food sources flourish only in certain areas at certain times of the year.

Feral horses, which are able to engage in social behaviour without human interference, typically organise themselves into two different kinds of groups, or bands, within the herd. One, commonly called the family band, consists of several mares, their foals and one or more stallions. If there are several stallions associated with the family band, the most dominant stallion copulates more than do the more subordinate ones. The other type of band, commonly referred to as the bachelor group (see p. 38), consists entirely of males.

Feral herd size tends to vary with population density and quality of forage. For example, on the eastern coast of the United States, in Shackleford Banks, herd sizes average around thirteen where there are eleven horses per square kilometre (about $^1/_3$ square mile). In parts of the Nevada Desert, where there are ten square kilometres (four square miles) per horse, there are seldom more than four in a group. There are a few exceptionally large herds that have been described in behavioural studies, although these are not truly feral. The largest of these social groups appear to be in Canada, where herds of working ponies that are seasonally managed on a free-living basis gather in groups of thirty or more.

I. Intelligence

Behavioural scientists are often quizzed on the relative intelligence of various domestic species. The usual response is to indicate the futility of the question, because not only are there numerous definitions of intelligence but there is also no single means of testing brain power that can impartially compare one species with another. For instance, some authorities argue that intelligence is measured by the extent to which an animal uses prior experience to solve new problems. Others insist that the ratio of brain weight to body weight is the key unit of cerebral power. Ultimately, intelligence means different things to different species, and so to attempt to compare the relative mental agility of two different fauna will always be unproductive.

Some say that to tolerate being ridden, with all the potential discomfort that may be expected when a thoughtless or ham-handed rider is on board, graphically illustrates how dull horses are. Others point out that they are so gregarious that they put up with humans because they see them as dominant companions. This could be a useful way of understanding horses' submission to bossiness on the part of riders – in horse-to-horse terms tyranny and dictatorships are seen as tolerable by subordinate individuals.

Problem-solving, in a behavioural test called a T-maze, is used to compare intelligence between one horse and another. It has been shown with this sort of technique that the discriminatory ability of youngsters can be enhanced by previous handling, although this may be on account of a reduced fear of novelty rather than a better-developed brain. That is to say, horses that have previously encountered humans and handling facilities may spend less time staring at them in a T-maze than a completely naive control group exposed to them for the first time during a test. Such tests have to be well designed to avoid their becoming more to do with memory than with intelligence. The two are so closely interwoven that many people believe that it is not possible to have one without the other.

If brain-to-body-weight ratio is relied upon as an index of intelligence, the horse emerges as almost level pegging with the turtle – which comes as a shock to fans of Champion the Wonderhorse or Mr Ed! Others simply point out that turtles are very intelligent when it comes to being turtles, and that to compare them with horses is as futile as comparing horses with humans because their brains have developed in different ways.

J. Jumping

Horses have evolved to avoid obstacles rather than to jump them. This truth is greeted with dismay by show-jumping fans and by the exponents of loose schooling, who believe that some horses regard jumping as a form of play. The fact is that horses that jump without riders in this way often have to be *taught* to do so, which suggests that they may be doing what they have to do to avoid the schooling-whip, not because they actively enjoy it. Perhaps evolutionists and show-jumpers are both right. It is possible that artificial selection has enhanced the ability of horses to clear fences and also selected those that enjoy doing so.

The anatomical mechanics involved when a horse jumps a fence are more or less the same as when he takes a gallop stride. Regardless of whether he is clearing a barrier or a ditch, his technique involves raising the forelegs while continuing to propel the body forward, with a final push that is achieved by full extension of the hindlegs. A good jump jockey moves accordingly to allow his horse to apply this method as naturally as possible. The head position of horses taking jumps while being loose-schooled tells us a great deal about how they size up a fence and how they decide when and where in the approach they should take off. Given the choice, most horses hold their heads up from the vertical – that is, in a position that purists might describe as being 'off the bit'. Struggling with a horse to keep his head tucked in when he approaches is therefore unlikely to help build his confidence, especially since he cannot properly focus on the jump as he advances unless he is able to alter the tilt of his head at will.

Jumping is obviously not achieved with equal success by all horses. Some clear obstacles with a natural 'bascule', while others have to struggle to achieve this smooth flexing of the back if they are not given systematic schooling. There are also those that never show any aptitude for jumping, despite having the required conformation for it. For many horses it is the appearance of a show jump rather than its height that proves the greatest obstacle. Many people believe that horses react to a new jump in the same way as to a potential predator, but if this were so one would expect them to refuse to approach the jump at all rather than simply to refuse to jump over it. Whether or not the jump is perceived as such a direct threat, the reasons for refusal can certainly involve fear. These possibilities are discussed more fully in Part Three.

Horses jumping free in a feral situation approach an obstacle one at a time, with the more experienced and therefore bolder horses tackling the problems before their younger herd-mates take on the challenge. Not only does this show the novices how to clear the obstacle but it also means that any danger on the far side can be exposed and dealt with by older horses. Each takes his time with the hazard and clears it with a minimum of pressure from the rear. It is interesting to note that when we ask racehorses to jump we expect them to do so as a group, and it is believed that this is what accounts for many of the falls we see on race-courses. It is not so much a lack of skill or stamina as the lack of space, that causes the horrific spills and injuries. The herd effect is what drives horses along together with so little regard for safety, and it is also this that teaches so many young hunters to clear fences at speed. The advantages of using school-masters in the training of youngsters cannot be overemphasised as a means of introducing novel fence designs and brightly coloured fillers.

K. Killing

There are very few cases in feral horse studies that involve one horse killing another, but infanticide – the killing of foals by stallions – has been recorded in groups of Przewalski horses kept in zoos. The problem here is that we cannot be certain whether it is the environment that is prompting the behaviour or whether it is a part of the horse behaviour repertoire, or ethogram. The horses responsible for the killing were stallions that were new to the group, and the victims were all unrelated male foals. This suggests that the behaviour has some parallels with infanticide in lions, which is understood to be a means of promoting the genes of the male that has most recently acceded to breeding rights within a pride. As with lions, the attacks by the Przewalski stallions were described as mauling of the head and neck that led to brain damage.

Combat between sparring stallions fighting for the breeding rights within a harem rarely ends with death. This is because when the signs of defeat are clear to the victor, he usually backs off to conserve his energy. All the same, fighting may result in injuries such as broken and kicked-out teeth. These traumatic consequences can jeopardise the stallion's survival some time after the fight itself – for example, by making him more vulnerable to predation or less able to feed effectively. Similarly, if blood poisoning or tetanus develops death may come from something as minor as a skin laceration.

Death at the time of combat does occur occasionally but, again, it is not documented for truly feral horses. Rather, such deaths seem to be confined to domesticated stallions which have entered into combat on being allowed to mix for the first time in the presence of mares in oestrus. In stallions, combat revolves around the forelimbs, which are flailed at the combatant in combination with attempts to knock him off balance. The greatest danger for a fighting stallion comes if he is sent crashing to the ground: it is at this point that the worst damage can be done – most commonly, legs can be broken. Permanent injuries make just as much sense from an evolutionary point of view as does killing the combatant – the fight is unlikely to be repeated if the vanquished horse is disabled.

L. Learning

Learning in horses takes the same forms as in other species, and a number of discrete processes are identified:

Habituation

When a stimulus is presented so many times that the instinctive response begins to disappear, *habituation* is said to have occurred. This adaptive process is seen in the initial training of any horse as it becomes less and less concerned about being bridled, saddled and ridden. Habituation is also the process employed by the mounted police when they aim to change their horses' response to all manner of roads, riots and rumpus into one of tolerance and calm rather than flight.

Conditioning

The other way horses learn is by a process called *conditioning*, which relies on the development of associations between stimuli and responses. Effectively, there are two sorts of conditioning: classical and operant.

In classical conditioning, a horse learns by associating an introduced signal with a natural (unconditioned) stimulus that evokes the given response. Take, for example, the association that develops when we call a horse's name while shaking a bucket of food. Its natural response is to travel towards the food, and so it begins to associate the sound of its name with the prospect of a snack. Operant conditioning, on the other hand, occurs when a horse's response to a given stimulus is positively or negatively reinforced by the trainer. Giving a food reward to a horse when he puts his head in a head-collar is a good example. In this case, the food is acting as a positive reinforcer because it is a pleasant event that increases the horse's willingness to put his head in the collar.

Unlike with modern dog and cat training the horse is still largely taught by negative reinforcement – that is, the introduction of an unpleasant event to increase his willingness to perform a given behaviour. This works because the horse learns that to perform a certain response is the only way of avoiding or escaping the unpleasant event. For instance, he will learn to move away from the pressure of leg aids, or he will learn that slowing his speed will ease the force of the bit on his tongue.

Because the association time for horses is probably little more than a second, the pairing of stimuli and rewards must occur within this time frame. If we use rewards at the *end* of a successful schooling session, we are rewarding behaviours that occur as the horse winds down rather than anything he accomplished in the middle of the work-out. So we tend to rely on secondary reinforcers that can be used at a distance or when our hands are otherwise occupied. Verbal praise such as 'Good boy' is an example of a secondary reinforcer that rewards the horse *if* he has already learned to associate these words with a primary positive reinforcer such as food.

The other most important feature of horse learning is the process known as *extinction*, which occurs when a horse ceases to perform the learned response because of the absence of any reinforcement. For instance, if an attention-seeking horse has learned that he can demand food by nuzzling his owner, he will eventually stop if the owner consistently fails to supply the expected reward. However, in instances like this where the reinforcement has been positive, the behaviour often undergoes an increase in frequency before it is extinguished. This is why, when behaviour therapy is used to achieve extinction, unwanted behaviours sometimes appear to get worse before they get better. Extinction can be enhanced by presenting a problem stimulus while the horse is engaged in an activity that is incompatible with the unwelcome response. This is known as counter-conditioning. An example of this approach is the

GENERAL
RELATIVITY
ALBERT EINSTEIN   Staub

The horse can teach itself.

use of tape-recordings of low levels of aversive noise, played near feed buckets while fearful horses are eating their concentrate ration. Because running away from noise means leaving the food, a new response to the stimulus can be acquired.

Owners should remember that they are not the only ones who can train the horse: he can teach himself. Learned behaviours that develop without the owner's awareness are often the thorniest problems to tackle. The key to understanding behaviours that have appeared spontaneously is to identify the mechanism that reinforces them. For example, until we fully understand the reward processes involved in the performance of *stereotypies* (which used to be called 'stable vices'), we will never be able to develop effective strategies to eliminate them. Moreover, with any unwelcome behaviour, it is not sufficient to remove the problem without giving the horse an alternative behaviour pattern to follow under the same initiating circumstances. For this reason, crib-biters cannot be effectively treated if they are not given the opportunity to forage, which provides an alternative outlet for their oral needs.

Social learning
As you can see, learning is one of the most complex areas of horse psychology and certainly one which merits further research. Our group at the University of Bristol veterinary school has recently examined the horses' ability to learn from one another. This process, known as *social learning*, has been described in many species but has not been demonstrated experimentally in the horse.

We trained a cob called Dylan to always eat out of a black and white striped bucket rather than a neighbouring yellow one, when given the choice. With a love of food that he shares with so many cobs, Dylan became a very reliable demonstrator. Next, twelve visiting horses and ponies were tested to see how they responded to the same arrangement of buckets, once six of them had seen Dylan's demonstration twenty times – we called them the 'test' group – while the remaining six were the 'control' group. When the test horses were allowed to make a choice, their approach to the pair of buckets was much quicker than the control horses'. Thus the results showed that horses that had witnessed Dylan's choice had learned something from the demonstration, using information from him to enhance their foraging behaviour. However, the choice of the striped or the yellow bucket made by the test group was random; as was the control group's. So they had not learned the finer discrimination between the two buckets. Compared with other species that have been tested for the ability to learn discrimination in this way, such as chickens, our horses did not fare very well.

It is possible that the experiment was not designed well enough to allow discriminative social learning. Perhaps the buckets were too far away from the observing horses, or perhaps Dylan's backside eclipsed their view! Either way, I am confident that one day someone will devise a demonstration system that is more user-friendly for observer horses, and that evidence of the insight one horse can gain from watching, smelling and listening to another will become clearer. My reason for believing that the transmission of information between horses is likely revolves around the fact that they are such social creatures. They must have evolved to gather information by observing other members of the same species in close proximity.

M. Memory

Horses have a remarkable memory, as any equine veterinary surgeon will confirm. The way that many horses respond when the vet comes into the box to deliver the annual vaccination booster provides a useful example. This sort of aversion is a learned behaviour that takes a very long time to become extinguished. It seems, therefore, that the best way to ingrain a response on a horse's memory is to use punishment – and, even better, to use it intermittently. This is not necessarily humane, so I am not so much advocating it as using it to illustrate why some learned behaviours take so long to disappear. The example that springs to mind involves vets who can evoke lifelong mistrust in some horses because their intermittent appearances make them unpredictable.

We all learn from our mistakes, but some animals have fewer chances to make mistakes than others. Let's consider, for a moment, any wild carnivore involved with any wild herbivore in a hunter-and-prey situation. If the carnivore makes a mistake it is likely to live to hunt again, but if the herbivore makes a mistake it is more likely to have to say a rapid prayer before departing to meet its maker. This means that, especially in frightening situations, horses as prey have to capitalise on any learning opportunity and make certain that they remember how they survived.

Memory is important for the survival of the foal every time he feeds from his mother, but, strangely, it is not *his* memory that is crucial here but that of his dam. She compares the scent of the foal that appears at her flank asking for milk with the memory of the scents she smelled at the time of his birth. If the two smells match one another and further visual and auditory cues help to confirm recognition, the mare will happily allow feeding to proceed; if not, then she will send the pretender packing and begin to search for her own youngster.

Memory is the key to effective learning, and horses seem to be motivated to store relevant information especially about potential food sources and potential threats. This is why these are the reinforcers that are most effective in inculcating a desired behaviour. Likewise, food and potential threats are the reinforcers that tend to be involved when a horse teaches *himself* a particular behaviour pattern. Negative experiences as a foal often appear to affect behaviour years later. While this means that tremendous care should be taken with the handling of foals, it does not imply that they are better off being left in the paddock. As we have seen in Chapter 2, exposing foals to positive experiences can facilitate learning in later life.

Pattern discrimination, which involves the horse being presented with patterns drawn on cards, is the test most commonly used to study equine memory. The two patterns are consistently presented together as a pair, with a reward being associated with just one of them. The position of the rewarding pattern is altered with successive presentations, so that the horse is not simply learning that good things are more likely to materialise on either the left or the right. Once reliable discrimination is achieved, the horse is rested until the retest; this could be months later, although the most interesting results are obtained when the percentage of correct pattern selection is plotted against time. The first month is when most of the memory loss occurs (approximately 10 per cent of the information); any subsequent forgetting of how to do the task is minimal. Intriguingly, fat horses make more mistakes in visual discrimination tests than thin ones. It has been suggested that this finding indicates that fat horses are less motivated to work for a food reward, not that they are less intelligent.

The phenomenal memory of horses can be put to good advantage in their general training. For example, early handling has been shown to enhance the learning ability of youngsters – an important fact for trainers. Many experienced horsefolk teach their horses fundamental lessons as youngsters and then turn them out to mature. This is an ideal approach where time and labour are limited, since early handling improves the uptake of information in later training sessions and is rarely forgotten. It has even been suggested that this training-followed-by-turn-out sequence is the only way that some horses can properly assimilate information. The system relies on the phenomenon of latent learning, which means that horses actually process the associations that we have presented them with even in the absence of the key stimuli.

N. Nuzzling

The first time a new-born foal searchs for a nipple, the elevation and extension of the head and neck, along with a characteristic protrusion of the tongue, herald the desire for milk. The foal is directed by subtle cues such as the direction of his mother's hair growth on her flank and his instinct to reach upwards into a darkened region on her underside. Some mares guide this nuzzling process by assuming a position that enables the foal, just by reaching forward, to find the teat. Even if he is not lucky enough to have such a helpful mother, the average foal finds nourishment within two hours. Only when the teat has been successfully located and his hunger satisfied can he begin to investigate his environment. After each subsequent foray he returns to his mother to feed, and nuzzling is part of the behaviour he adopts to ensure a welcoming reception at the milk bar.

When a hungry foal appears at his mum's flank looking for a milky feed, he does not simply bowl up, attach himself to a nipple and start guzzling. Some might say that this approach would not work because it is rude! In fact, it would simply be ineffectual. Milk does not passively lie in the udder waiting to be drained; it is retained in saccules and caverns within the tissues of the mammary gland and is only released by a process known as 'milk let-down'. Foals nuzzle their mothers as part of a ritualised sequence of preliminary behaviour – an essential overture because it is this that stimulates the hormone cascade which leads to the release of milk. So nuzzling is one of the accumulation of cues that are required for effective nursing. Others include the sight of the approaching foal tossing his head and laying back his ears. An exchange of maternal and infant nickerings is also common before bouts of nursing. There is thought to be an additional, non-nutritional, role to sucking behaviour which seems to meet the need of young animals to be comforted. Many people believe that, regardless of the quantity of milk consumed, sucking helps the foal to feel cared for. This may explain why foals occasionally suck other parts of their dams and sometimes the dry teats of other females.

The nuzzling behaviour shown by hungry foals is an example of care-seeking behaviour. Another can be seen in affiliated horses at pasture that elicit allogrooming (see p. 144) from their field-mates by well timed use of the appealing nuzzle. So here we have two instances of horses communicating their demands to other horses by nuzzling them. It should be of little surprise to us that they use the same technique to pester their human companions for the scratch or the treat that they have learned to expect. This behaviour is usually reinforced by the delivery of a reward, since most well trained humans who are used to being around horses make the appropriate response!

O. Olfaction

Olfaction, the sense of smell, in horses provides some of the most valuable information about their environment. Most of the nerve endings responsible for smell are found at the back of the horse's elongated nasal cavity. The bones here are scrolled on top of one another, which increases the surface area both for smelling and for heat loss, which is the nose's other main job in horses.

The head-to-head exchange of odours that occurs when two horses meet highlights the species' reliance on the sense of smell . . . It is their way of gathering information about one another's gender, maturity and recent foraging. Smells can also speak of recent fear and exertion, as well as current health status. In the case of prospective sexual partners, further sniffing is conducted all over the body: in this way the stallion uses his olfactory powers to determine the reproductive status of mares in his harem. Eleven months later, as already mentioned, the mares use the same sense to confirm that the foals drinking from their flanks are their own and not freeloaders.

Olfaction also plays a key role in flight and defence, being an important means of gaining early warning of an approaching threat. There is an unmistakable muskiness to most carnivorous animals, and this is probably the smell that horses use to identify predators. It appears that tell-tale odours can be detected by smell even when their bearers have attempted elaborate camouflaging tactics such as rolling in dung!

Piles of dung are an unmistakable sign that horses have been in an area. Their presence is often acknowledged by horses on a hack by their dropping their own calling-card on top of the existing one. The olfactory component is not the only one used in this scenario, since it appears that the existing monument is spotted some way off by the approaching horse, and this visual stimulus helps to prepare his bowels to drop faeces in close proximity to the intended site. A similar mimicry effect can be seen with urine: the smell of one horse's urine on the ground seems to provoke others to make their mark – the smell of previous urination appears to be what makes horses so reliably urinate when brought into a strange stable, for instance.

Leg chestnuts seem to stimulate tremendous interest when they are peeled off one horse and presented to another. These horny growths are thought to be vestiges of the evolutionary process that reduced weight-bearing in equids from a five-toe to a single-toe apparatus. There are other remnants of toes in the skeleton of the modern horse's lower limb, and it is not clear why these, unlike the chestnuts, leave no sign on the outside of the skin. Chestnuts are also a site of special interest when horses meet and greet. Vets in many countries use photographs of these crumbly outcrops to identify horses for legal purposes, because their shape and contours are unique to each individual horse. It is possible that their scent is also a uniquely coded 'fingerprint' that only other horses can unscramble. Another intriguing feature is that it is not uncommon for horses in bonded pairs to trim one another's chestnuts by chewing them back to the level of the surrounding skin.

P. Play

Although not confined to foals, some of the most interesting features of equine play are seen in immature animals. This is why play is thought to have a major role in the social,

Horseplay is an enjoyable sort of pastime for the learning foal.

emotional and physiological development of young horses and ponies. Indeed, horseplay is an enjoyable sort of pastime for the learning foal. It has been suggested that the amount of play performed by any horse is related to the availability of energy from its diet. According to this theory, foals in the feral state, having a high-energy food source, show lots of play behaviour, while adults having to forage on low-quality grazing show very little because it is too costly. In domestic environments, which provide high-energy foods, play returns to the repertoire of behaviour even for adult horses.

Solitary foals are regularly spotted playing. This usually takes the form of exaggerated bursts of speed and general cavorting, but the pawing and mouthing of inanimate objects like sticks and twigs are also thought to be a form of play behaviour. Some observers have suggested that the function of mouthing could be to develop the selectivity and dexterity of the musculature of the tongue and lips. But it is difficult to see what immediate gratification a foal gets from this sort of play because, unlike with carnivorous youngsters, catching hold of toys would appear to be irrelevant to an animal that has only to mouth immobile vegetation as an adult. Whatever the immediate reward a foal can create for himself by this sort of play, though, it may well help to explain how the manipulation of man-made environmental features like stable doors and light switches can be achieved in later life!

Play between the foal and his mother forms the main social activity in his first month of life. It is he who appears to do almost of all the playing, while his mother's role in the games seems generally to be to stand still and tolerate abuse. The foal's mouthplay is rather rough during the first two weeks of life, but then mellows to give way to more gentle nibbling that invites the dam to engage in mutual grooming activity. The first fortnight of life tends to be the crucial time for bonding between foals and their dams. Only after this does play between peers begin to develop.

Some of the most fascinating examples of play between horses are observed between foals and other young horses. The use of toys, as described above for solitary foals, has also been recorded in groups of youngsters. One particularly appealing – or perhaps particularly kinky – story involves a yearling colt and a yearling filly that were spotted playing in a paddock one afternoon. The male seized hold of a flat plastic feed pan and started tossing it around. Then, with the pan between his teeth, he walked up to his female companion and started spanking her quarters with it! As you can imagine, this was not considered amusing by the filly on the receiving end of the flagellation and she soon sent him packing.

More conventional play between peers involves chasing, mutual grooming and play-fighting. The particular combination of these components depends on the gender of the participants, with play-fighting being rare among pairs of fillies. In fact, play of any sort is more common among male pairs than in any group that includes a female foal.

The other kind of play that merits consideration is that between a foal and adults other than its mother. For instance, colts have been recorded pulling at stallions' manes and being tolerated while performing all sorts of apparently cheeky behaviour. But this all ends when the young male reaches his third year and the harem stallion begins to regard him as a sexual rival. It is not clear what helps the stallion to sense this change in his male offspring, but olfactory cues would appear to be the most likely mechanism involved.

Q. Quidding

When a horse drops his food he is said to be *quidding*. This rather quaint term describes any loss of food from his mouth. So it is not terribly useful, since tooth loss, nerve damage, pain or unpalatable food may all be present when the behaviour happens. Furthermore, there are older manuals of horse management that regard quidding as a 'vice', despite the fact that the same books recognise many dental causes for it. This is another unfortunate misuse of the word 'vice' because it suggests that the affected horse has some sort of malicious intent. Clearly, this could not be further from the truth for a horse with tooth loss or nerve damage, who may lose food from his mouth because he is simply unable to chew without some fall-out.

When a horse quids, it behoves the owner to establish the cause because of the possible pain involved and the resultant food wastage and weight loss. There are a number of clues that can help to discern one cause of quidding from another. For instance, oral discomfort as a manifestation of molar disease rarely involves both sides of the mouth equally, and so it often produces a fine head tilt – which is an attempt on the part of the horse to let gravity send food into the healthier side of the mouth. Such dental problems usually involve molars that are growing unevenly and have developed painful spurs, which catch the lining of the cheek with each attempt to chew. With more generalised pain, hard rations are completely rejected in favour of softened foods and fresh forage, and the behaviour associated with the quidding of unpalatable food tends to include movement of the tongue in an attempt to evacuate the food from the mouth. Choices that a horse makes in his feeding behaviour can thus tell us a great deal about his health.

Some owners report that their horses are bored with one sort of food, and they can only improve appetite by offering alternatives. Unpalatable food will often be totally rejected, especially if the motivation to eat is not at its highest. This explains why cosseted, picky feeders with a wide choice of food throw it all over the place, while Shetland ponies scraping an existence on the coast near Orkney can be seen tucking into seaweed and not wasting a morsel. But being bored with the food is rarely a reason for it being taken into the mouth and then discarded: where the motivation to feed is low the horse rarely bothers even to bite into his ration.

Unfamiliar food may be tested with considerable caution by some horses; indeed, the novelty of certain flavours can cause temporary rejection. This equine mistrust of novel foodstuffs is recognised by experienced horse owners, who usually adopt a *weaning* strategy that reduces the old food over a period of days while at the same time gradually introducing the new. 'Weaning' is an excellent label for this process, since there is no more dramatic change in the nutrition of any mammal than when he stops drinking his dam's milk and changes to solids. If it were possible to make changes as gradually as they occur in Nature, food-rejection problems would be very rare indeed.

R. Range

The size and stocking density of a range is closely related to the availability of key resources, including grazing sites, water-holes, shade, wind-breaks and refuges from insects. Home ranges can vary in area from under one to nearly fifty square kilometres (twenty square miles).

When we speak of 'homing' in horses, we are referring to their ability to relocate their home range with all its familiar sights and smells. Indeed, it is thought that ranges are identified, rather than delineated, by marking methods. For example, stud piles (faecal accumulations made by stallions) in domestic ranges tend to be used as marks within, rather than at the borders of, a home range. In feral contexts, these monuments appear in communal areas such as paths that are used by more than one overlapping harem. Domestic stallions do their best to mimic this behaviour pattern by leaving their stud piles close to fence lines, apparently in a bid to signal to horses on the other side of the fence.

Defence of the home range depends largely on the time of year. The presence of females in oestrus can alter the attitude of both mares and stallions within the harem to the approach of strangers. One may distinguish between a *territory*, which involves the concept of land ownership, and a *range*, which encompasses ownership of resources and of dependants. Therefore, the extent to which a range is defended depends also on the degree of overlap with other bands of horses. It is in areas of overlap that most agonistic activity takes place between bands, especially during the mating season. The same process is apparent in domestic situations, with part of the fence line being the favoured latrine area when a new horse is introduced to a field adjoining an established group of horses.

One of the most striking differences between the ways that feral and domestic horses live is in the size of their home ranges. The reduced range available for a group of domestic animals means that population density is increased, with the result that each individual within the group is more likely to encounter aggression because it regularly invades another horse's personal space.

S. Sleep

The way in which a horse sleeps depends to a great extent on its age. For example, foals tend to sleep on their sides or flat out on the ground, while adults prefer to sleep standing up. Similarly, the time spent sleeping is dependent on age, with youngsters spending a third of their day asleep whereas in adults this figure falls to no more than 5 per cent.

In horses, light sleep (classified by researchers as slow wave sleep) is more common than deep sleep (rapid eye movement sleep). This is because a standing position cannot be employed in deep REM sleep, although it is possible in SWS. Sleep makes up only a fraction of rest behaviour, which also includes drowsing and idling. Horses have been observed to spend 85 per cent of the day in wakefulness or drowsing, with the proportion of drowsiness increasing in a single individual when it is in a protected environment.

Age and environment are not the only factors to influence sleep patterns since fatigue is another important element. Diet also plays a role. For instance, research shows that horses given hay-based rations spend 20 per cent more of their time in deep sleep on the ground than when they are offered oat-based diets. Since this suggests that a high-energy, low-fibre diet reduces daily sleeping time, one might expect sleep to become a less popular pastime in the summer months, when the best food is available. In fact, this does not happen because sun is another important influence on sleep patterns. Horses sleep while sunbathing for up to thirty minutes at a time. Next time you see a horse sunning himself, watch how meticulously he selects a spot and orientates one side of his body to maximise its exposure to the sun's rays.

Naturally, sunbathing is less readily available to horses in the winter, but even if this were not the case few feral horses would have sufficient time to enjoy it because foraging is the obligatory activity at this time of the year. Apart from fatigue, the only other important influence on sleep behaviour in horses is the sight of other horses dozing off. As we saw in Chapter 2, the process whereby one animal performing a behaviour seems to trigger the same behaviour in others – such as the infectious yawn that travels through groups of humans at board meetings – is known as 'social facilitation'. Although this seems to have a potent effect on almost all the horses in a group, it is usual to find at least one band member that does not succumb; he or she is the watch-horse for the group – a role that, thankfully, is shared.

Because they are so much lighter than adult horses, foals can sleep for extended periods on the ground, which means that the lungs can be ventilated properly and blood can be pumped through the lung tissues. As a horse's body weight increases, the heart finds difficulty in pushing blood through the lung tissue when he lies on one side. Thus lying on the brisket is the favoured posture if he elects to sleep on the ground.

Because escape from predators relies on a quick getaway as well as agility and stamina, the horse has evolved to reach top speeds rapidly from a standing rather than a lying start. As evidenced by the groaning that often accompanies it, getting up from the ground involves considerable effort for all horses simply because they are so heavy. So it makes sense for them to sleep standing up. The ligaments and tendons within their lower limbs are assembled in such a way as to allow them to stand and rest without using muscular contraction. The absence of any muscular effort means that sleep while standing is both possible and quite comfortable.

T. Taste

Horses have taste buds all over their tongues, and also at the back of their mouths in the region known as the oropharynx. Taste is the main sense that they use to avoid eating toxic substances and to regulate their salt intake. On an anecdotal level, we know that the salt content of substances can certainly be detected by horses, because they travel considerable distances to salt-lick locations. Furthermore, as already mentioned, horses grazed beside seashores are known to ingest seaweeds and occasionally sea-water, which suggests that their ability to regulate sodium is better than for other minerals.

Our understanding of taste in animals is limited, because it varies considerably both between individuals and between one species and the next. In addition, it is difficult to devise good tests of taste. One of the most straightforward ways of studying it is to offer horses water with different concentrations of various flavours, and then record their behaviour in response to these solutions. Experience of flavours associated with previous diets can interfere with the results, so foals are the best subjects for these studies. Although we are aware that horses can detect salt in water, it is the foals in these tests that have helped us to determine what concentration of salt causes them to reject the water. In this way we can build up a mental picture of what kinds of flavours horses are especially sensitive to, and also relate it to other species. The ability to discern sweetness is tested with sugar, sourness with vinegar, and bitterness with quinine.

Using this experimental design, research has shown that horses are strikingly similar to sheep in their responses to all four flavours. Essentially this means that, while low concentrations of sugar can be detected by equids, tastes that are salty, sour and bitter have to be in high concentrations to cause aversion. This explains, for example, why horses are better than humans at coping with bitter foods. Despite their sensitivity to sweetness, horses and ponies cannot discriminate the calorific content of a dietary component and do not favour particular species of grasses because of the energy content. Their preference for certain types of grass species seems to arise from the blend of flavours and the percentage of water that they contain rather than their nutritional value. Early studies into these preferences has shown, for instance, that horses select white clover and timothy rather than red clover and meadow foxtail.

U. Urination

A straddled stance is adopted by horses of all ages and both sexes when they urinate, to avoid wetting the hindlegs. This may be why they will usually refrain from urinating on concrete, and aim to position themselves in windy weather so that the urine is carried away from them by the breeze. There are even stories of horses that prefer to halt at stormwater drains in order to urinate when being ridden out on the roads.

Mares and stallions urinate in slightly different ways. The straddled stance, for example, is more pronounced in the mare and during oestrus is maintained while she goes through a clitoris-winking display. Her usual rate of urination is approximately once every four hours, but during her season it is more frequent, with more than twenty urinations in an hour being far from unusual. By lowering her pelvis a mare in season is also able to squat. The characteristics of urination at this time are important visual cues for any stallion that may escort her; stallions can often be seen trotting over to oestrous mares as soon as they have finished urinating. The arousing effect that urine from an oestrous mare can have on a stallion seems to be especially marked in younger males, and is put to good advantage at studs that collect semen for artificial insemination purposes. Young stallions will often refuse to mount phantom, or dummy, mares unless these are first sprinkled with urine collected from mares in oestrus.

Urination on to piles of faeces is a pattern of behaviour that develops in colts and fillies as they mature. It seems unlikely that urination is used as a territorial marking procedure, since territories are rare in horses and, furthermore, horses do not typically urinate when they are first turned out into a new paddock.

As mentioned earlier, when a mare urinates in response to a faecal pile, she tends to do so without advancing to the actual dung spot. Her urine lands a body's length behind it, which can cause the latrine area to spread. A stallion, on the other hand, tends to approach a pile of faeces, investigate, and then walk on a little to stand over the pile in order to urinate on top of it. But this sort of behaviour pattern is generally displayed in response to the excrement of females. Entire males in the wild do not tend to urinate on communal stallion dung piles. During aggressive encounters between stallions, often in the vicinity of stud piles, urination is not a common feature of display as it is with dogs. Perhaps this is because it is not possible to urinate on the move: it would reduce the manoeuvrability and increase the vulnerability of the performer. It seems likely that a stallion reserves urine for marking the top of his mare's excrement, either to conceal her reproductive status or to signify that she is accompanied by a stallion.

It has been said that horses can be taught to perform almost any appropriate behaviour, and so the suggestion has been made that they can be house-trained in the same way as dogs. To do this successfully, of course, one would have to be with the horse for most of the day and night in order to be present during every elimination. The presence of the trainer is certainly important if the behaviours that we are aiming to promote are to be immediately reinforced and encouraged in specific contexts.

V. Vision

The horse's eye appeals to humans because it is so large. Indeed, relative to total body mass, horses are among the largest-eyed of all animals. This suggests that visual information is of tremendous importance to them but does not, in itself, explain what they are good at looking at. The vision of each species is refined to maximise the quantity of data important to its survival and quality of life. Take this broad example – whether long-sightedness or short-sightedness may have advantages for a given animal will depend on whether it survives by hunting or by escaping from hunters. We can learn a great deal about the world for which horses have evolved by considering how that world is perceived by horses themselves.

Some knowledge of vision in the horse can be gained from studying the anatomy of its eye. However, this is a technique which has led to some confusion in the past, with the description of the so-called 'ramp retina'. For years this was an accepted feature of the equine eye, and it resulted in the suggestion that horses focus on objects at varying distances by tilting their heads up and down! However, this explanation was later discredited. The mistake had arisen because, instead of being studied *in vivo*, the horse eyes had been left on benches in dissection rooms before examination and had thus assumed a flattened back. A further example of inaccurate interpretation that can arise from studying the anatomy rather than the live animal involves colour vision. Early anatomists commented on the presence of cones in the retinas of horses, suggesting that these colour receptors were merely vestigial. Yet no one at the time had tested living horses for colour-blindness.

The alternative, or complementary, way to understand what a horse can see is to observe and test its behaviour in response to stimuli of different colours. The German researcher Bernhard Grzimek, who was working on horse vision in the 1950s (he is mentioned on p. 172 for his work on horses' recognition of shapes), was responsible for early experiments of this sort. He found that his experimental animals discriminated yellow panels best. The trouble is that when testing pigments of different wavelengths, one also has to control the amount of light reflected by the surface one has coloured – a particular problem with colours that are inherently bright, like yellow. Unfortunately, we cannot say to what extent his experimental design controlled for reflectance. Colours that can be matched for reflectance have been tested again recently, and scientists in the United States have shown that horses can discriminate blue and red from various shades of grey. They have suggested, therefore, that horses may be dichromats – that is, they see a world with these two colours as well as shades of black and white.

At night, when everything appears rather black and white, horses have better vision than man. This is probably because, like cats and dogs, they have a reflective film in their retina which helps to maximise the effect of any light that enters the eye. (Incidentally, this is why their eyes shine when a torch beam meets them at night.) The need for good nocturnal vision is related to the avoidance of predators rather than to the selection of good grazing. For the same reason, horses are acutely sensitive to moving objects in the lateral margins of their fields of vision. With its evolutionary origins as a predator-detector, this faculty for spotting peripheral motion tends to ring alarm bells even for many domesticated horses: these are the ones that flee from a perceived danger, then pull up some distance away, and only then turn their heads to get a better look.

The other feature of equine vision that merits particular note is the capacity to detect fine detail. This visual acuity has been demonstrated many times, but is best illustrated by the tale of Clever Hans, a horse that lived in Austria in the 1900s. He was studied by many scientists, who wanted to determine how he performed his celebrated feats of memory and arithmetic with such accuracy. The horse counted by pawing with a front foot, and when he arrived at the correct number he would stop, to the delight of his master and the assembled audience. Hans was just as accurate in the absence of his master – which seemed to rule out any kind of trickery. Many learned Austrian heads were scratched, until eventually someone suggested that an opaque screen be placed between Hans and his human observers. This done, a question was posed and the counting started. The counting continued, the answer was reached, but still the counting continued. The illusion did not work. What this experiment had demonstrated was that Hans had learned to detect the changes in body posture and breathing patterns that occurred in humans when they knew that he had counted for long enough; he had been trained to look for tiny visual clues that humans were unable to discern.

A present-day exponent of the role of equine visual acuity is the American horseman Monty Roberts, who highlights the importance of the way in which a horse reads human body language. Roberts quite rightly maintains that the non-linguistic area of horse-training is one that deserves tremendous consideration. He would probably suggest that it is via body language that a horse that is difficult to catch can detect whether the owner is trying to hide a head-collar!

Horses' reliance on good visual information begins in the earliest moments of life; indeed, sight seems to be the first sense they deploy. A remarkable feature of equine vision is the way in which, when compromised, it can be compensated for. There are any number of stories of horses and ponies that have successfully continued show-jumping careers long after the onset of cataracts, and sometimes even after the loss of one eye.

W. Weaning

Typically, colts depart from their family groups earlier than fillies. Because sexual activity arises earlier in males than in females, it is supposed that this trend promotes the dispersal of genes.

Weaning is a gradual process in nature, which is usually complete in weeks but occasionally only days before the next foal is born. However, even in free-ranging herds weaning can sometimes be quite abrupt, with mares suddenly avoiding their foals or threatening them when they approach to feed. Weaning is likely to be initiated by the discomfort associated with the foal's growing teeth and its tendency to spend so much more of the day gaining nourishment from forage than from the mare. One of the most important factors appears to be whether the mare is pregnant again. If she is, then weaning is a virtual certainty; if not, then she may continue nursing for a second summer. Rather quaintly, in free-ranging horses, if a suckling foal dies its dam will resume nursing her previous year's foal. In this way she enhances the viability of her genes, which she has already passed on to the surviving foal. One could also argue that it gives the mare both physical and emotional comfort.

Weaning in domestic environments can be the most stressful time in a horse's life. The separation of such a social creature from a bonded individual, in this case its mother, is known to cause a measurable rise in most physiological parameters of stress, including blood cortisol levels. The horses's close relative, the donkey, can even develop fatal metabolic diseases as a result of not eating, as a feature of what we might call 'pining'. In the light of these facts, many horse owners are now employing methods of weaning that have been shown to cause less dramatic rises in physiological stress. Of these, the most commonly used takes a group of mares and foals that have to be weaned, and instead of all the foals being removed into isolation at one time, the mares are removed one by one in a protracted process. The mare with the oldest foal is selected first, and when her offspring runs around searching for her he can resort, in her absence, to the company of his peers. When the searching behaviour is no longer evident in the first-weaned foals, the next mare can be removed, and so on, until just the foals remain in the paddock.

X. Xenophobia

In the feral horse, xenophobia, the fear of strangers, is a policy of mistrust with tremendous advantages. The possible gains from tolerating the presence of a strange horse, let alone a member of another species, are minimal. Animals in the wild do not rush up to one another offering gifts of food and affection. There is no animal equivalent of the Red Cross movement! This is why unhandled mountain ponies have to learn that food can be *given* to them by humans – they have no experience of another animal freely submitting a valuable resource.

There is therefore no reason why any wild animal should give an approaching stranger the benefit of the doubt. The distance a horse will allow an unfamiliar animal to approach without heading for the hills depends on the stranger's shape and on the horse's prior experience of creatures sharing that shape. The smell of the stranger, and specifically whether it smells as though it's a carnivore or not, seems particularly crucial at this point. This accounts for the prevalence of snorts when a horse approaches something strange; these exhalations help to clear the airways and enhance the wary animal's detection of all-important olfactory clues.

The acceptance of a stranger is made more likely if he gives out cues that are familiar and therefore reassuring. A strange horse approaching members of his own species will certainly be treated with mistrust but, unlike a hungry predator, he does not attempt to cloak his arrival. Instead, he advertises his presence with calls and dances that intrigue and provide reassurance. Once identified as a horse, the intruder has potential as a companion and as a prospective mate.

On the other hand, there are also threats associated with the arrival of an unfamiliar horse. For example, he can signal the loss of established mating partners and other limited resources like food and water. One can understand the ambivalence that may be directed towards a newly arrived member of the same species if one has ever been involved in a National Lottery syndicate! Despite the fact that larger groups have improved chances of success, additional partners in this sort of co-operative are sometimes mistrusted because they will share the benefits even though they have only recently started to contribute to the group's efforts. In the same way, animals invest in the fitness of the group because it improves their own genes' chances of success, and the novel individual brings with it new genes that may capitalise on the work already put in by existing herd members.

Y. Yawning

The typical horse yawn is very similar to that of other mammals, beginning with the mouth opening slightly followed by an enormous inhalation. The eyes often roll behind half-closed lids during the rest of the yawn, which is punctuated by exhalation. Yawning joins a horse's behavioural repertoire within twenty-four hours of birth, and is also recognised as a predictable part of stallion behaviour because it is a curiously common feature of their post-coital dismount!

The notion that the stretching of a muscle group is good for both flexibility and tone is as true for facial muscles as it is for leg and back muscles. Stretching improves blood flow, and therefore helps the circulation to flush away waste products from tired or stagnant muscle groups. Facial stretching is thought to be important for improving blood flow not only to the jaw muscles but to the head in general. Furthermore, many vets believe that its importance does not stop there, because it has been noted that horses in mild pain seem to yawn more often than completely relaxed horses. Why this should be is not clear – maybe the enhanced blood flow helps to release the body's own pain-killers from their reserves in the brain.

Other interesting instances of yawns that might seem out of place include the ones that happen as soon as the bridle is put on, and the ones that appear as part of stereotypic behaviour. Yawns associated with bridling arise because *arousal* is increasing in anticipation of work, in the same way that we might yawn as we get out of bed. So yawns that emerge during tacking up should not be regarded as a hint that the horse regards you as a dreadful bore! When he repeatedly yawns over the stable door in response to your arrival or to the departure of a stable mate, he is likely to be showing a stereotypic response to a stimulus that tends to bring with it a degree of frustration. For the same reason, some weavers will every so often throw a yawn into their repetitive sequence of head and shoulder movements.

In rare cases, repeated yawning can also be associated with pathological drowsiness in cases of encephalomyelitis, a form of brain damage, and in ragwort poisoning. However, the sight of two yawns in swift succession should never send the concerned owner racing to the nearest phone to call the vet! Yawning does not appear in isolation as a symptom of these disorders – there are a number of more graphic signs that alert owners to the onset of such grave illnesses.

Z. Zebra

No compiler of an alphabet of horse behaviour could resist grabbing the opportunity to use the letter Z to discuss the horse's cousin, the zebra. It has been said that we should be looking to the zebra for indications of *true* wild horse behaviour, since the feral populations have been generated from domesticated animals and therefore cannot be an accurate indicator of how equids have evolved to behave. Indeed, in the absence of any established population of Przewalski's horses, we may do well to study zebra herds for an insight into how a purely wild version of our stabled companions behaves. But having said that, we must bear in mind that there are some striking differences between horses and zebras. For example, horses and ponies have thirty-two pairs of chromosomes, while zebras have forty-four. Strangely, despite the difference in chromosome numbers, live hybrids have been born from crosses between the two species (although the offspring have all been sterile).

Leaving aside the genetic and anatomical differences, the behavioural similarities between the zebra and the horse seem to depend on which of the three zebra species one considers. Plains and mountain zebras organise themselves into small harem groups in much the same way as does *Equus caballus*. However, these groups live in large home ranges that overlap. The third species of zebra, Grevy's, tends to feed communally during the day but retreats into small bands at night. Furthermore, during the breeding season stallions of this species defend a defined mating territory, especially when it is occupied by a receptive female.

Despite the striking social differences, the zebra's

response to real predation offers an interesting model for behavioural scientists who aim to understand horse behaviour. For instance, when a zebra is brought down by hunting dogs, they hold it by the nose. This has led researchers to speculate that endorphin release, resulting from nose pain, may just occasionally give the prey sufficient analgesia to organise its escape. Naturally, escape is not possible in every episode of predation but, in theory, pain-stimulated pain relief is a physiological phenomenon that could be selected for.

Zoos with zebra-breeding programmes have been so hugely successful that they are now selling zebras to selected private homes. Although these creatures are traditionally regarded as resolutely intractable, some horse trainers are beginning to have dramatic successes with them. In fact, some observers have been so impressed that they have speculated that zoos may have selected for good temperament, which would explain why zebras are more biddable than they used to be. This cannot be the whole story, though. Etchings that show Lord Rothschild's zebras drawing carriages around Regent's Park at the turn of the century and reports of their use in Africa as pack-animals suggest that these animals have always been trainable. For this reason, I am inclined simply to credit the trainers in question with the ability to manipulate equine behaviour, rather than to dismiss the current examples as the product of long-term captivity.

Part Three

WHY DOES MY HORSE . . . ?

Having discussed the importance of a thoughtful approach to problem-solving in horse management and considered the A to Z of normal horse behaviour, we can now begin to examine some examples of unwelcome behaviours that *Equus caballus* performs when stabled and when ridden.

As a boy I was told that if a horse reared with me on board, I should smash an egg on his poll to make him think he had just cracked his head open on a beam. I now know that, armed with a thorough understanding of horse behaviour rather than a box of eggs, we can improve on this sort of wisdom. While traditional techniques may offer quicker resolutions to some of the problems that we shall consider in this section, they often tend to generate fear and eliminate the horse's own resourcefulness. Furthermore, they are generally less safe and less humane. Horses that are compelled to perform a given behaviour often resist, and resistance can turn into violent equine tantrums.

If *safety* is not considered first and foremost, such tantrums can lead to tears before bedtime – and I mean a *hospital* bed. In my opinion, any approach to horse-handling should always make safety its first priority. Therefore, throughout Part Three you will notice that the accent is on modification rather than compulsion.

The strategies I recommend are not the only ones that can be adopted for a specific problem; they should be regarded simply as examples of behavioural therapy that have been shown to work in practice. Each horse and his or her owner represent a package of individual experience and sensitivity that merits a great deal of thought in the design of each therapeutic programme. It is very often the owner, working from the behaviourist's blueprint, who is the best person to tailor the action plan to suit the specific situation. I usually find that, once the principles of behaviour modification are established and the cause of the trouble is identified, a sensible strategy can be arrived at that will eliminate any reward for the unwanted behaviour and reinforce a more desirable response in the animal.

What follows is a selection of the questions I receive every day as veterinary surgeon, riding instructor and equine behaviourist. Some of them refer to normal features of horse behaviour that have provoked intrigue rather than concern, while others involve behaviour patterns that are serious and potentially dangerous for both horses and humans. I have also included in this section features of normal horse behaviour that did not merit sufficient priority to be discussed in Part Two.

The questions come from owners who want to know more about why their horses and ponies behave as they do. All names have been changed to protect the innocent! When answering postal questions, I usually make the following assumptions: that the owner has a co-operative veterinarian, an ability to break with tradition and a rudimentary dollop of horse sense. Beyond that, the two main prerequisites in any animal-training recipe are patience and consistency. Without these ingredients, this book would be as useless as a chocolate fire-guard.

WHY DOES MY HORSE?

A

Attacking
Horses exhibit aggression towards humans in the presence
of food in the same way as they would towards other horses.
Even though feral horses spend so much of their day grazing, they do not do so passively. While to the casual observer
they seem to be munching and marching through grassland
to no particular purpose, they are in fact sorting through the
available forage in search of the choicest areas of herbage on
which to expend their energies. Furthermore, chewing itself
is not without its cost, so it makes sense for horses to be
selective. Once they have secured a worthwhile patch, they
will be motivated to defend it from the unwelcome attentions of subordinate herd members. Similarly, in winter or
when food is scarce, for survival's sake it's a question of
every horse for itself. Consequently they defend, rather than
share, what nourishment they can find.

It is this defence of one's resources – an everyday part
of normal horse behaviour – that is unacceptable when it
rebounds on to humans. As we bring food to our equine
charges, we rarely take time to view the ritual of its delivery
from the horses' angle. We may note that the aggression is
worse when a horse is expecting its concentrate feed rather
than its forage, and also when it is engaged in a lot of work
– both times when the domesticated horse's motivation and
need to access the resource are at their greatest. Dog owners
who expect their canine companions to sit patiently before
charging into the feed bowl will continue to be surprised by
their horses' quite different table manners. Dogs' forbear-
ance in this situation may derive from the fact that dog
behaviour has its roots in the social world of the wolf, which
has a number of placatory and begging strategies in its
repertoire since these help to bond mother and cubs before

she gives them food by regurgitation. Obviously, no equivalent exists in the spectrum of equine behaviour. Neither is there any place in feral horse behaviour for deference. Feral horses take the view that if something is worth defending they should defend it – and if a subordinate has something worth taking they should depose him. The main point here is that, once it has arrived at the spot where it is normally consumed, that food resource becomes the property of the horse. This is why food aggression peaks as the human holding the food approaches the manger.

Question
I have a two-and-a-half-year-old Thoroughbred filly called Mott. She was purchased from an amateur breeder, where she had been kept with her dam. I ferried them both to my yard to wean them. One week after I bought her, Mott had an accident in some barbed wire and required more than twenty stitches in her near-side hind cannon. The re-dressings which ensued over the following six weeks involved a lot of pain. She became quite resentful of the twitch, and her hindlegs became more and more sensitive. Six months later, I sold the dam and bought an aged female donkey as a companion for Mott. They seem to like one another and often graze happily side by side.

However, to this day Mott hates having her legs touched and so this is a problem when I try to pick up her feet. Over the last few months things have gone from bad to worse. I have found that I can only take food away from her with great difficulty and even have trouble delivering fresh hay and concentrates to her in the stable. She has started to lunge at me whenever I go into the stable. The other day she backed me up against the wall of the loose-box and let fly with both hindlegs. Despite the fact that she didn't actually hit me, I was very shaken and, picking myself up off the floor, went to fetch a dressage whip from the yard. Once I had found the whip, I went back to her box and gave her a sound wallop, but I can't help feeling that she is now far from trustworthy. In the field, she is aggressive towards humans who approach her while she is grazing and often chases them over the nearest fence. She also tends to rear when she sees the lead rope and is generally becoming difficult to lead around. I am considering sending her away to be disciplined but am reluctant to leave the donkey on her own. Why do you think Mott has become so unmanageable, and what would you recommend I do with her?

Answer

There are several steps that would he helpful in modifying your relationship with Mott, and I would advise you to take them sooner rather than later. The longer you leave it before acting, the harder it will be to change her behaviour because she will have received more rewards for the unwelcome responses – I will explain what I mean in a moment – and she will also have become a stronger force to be reckoned with.

Mott has learned to be aggressive as a reliable means of getting you to do what she wants. For example, she gets rid of you when you deal with her hindlegs, and she has learned to send you packing when there is food around. It's time to consider how her manipulative behaviour patterns can be eliminated and replaced with safer and more sociable responses.

First of all, Mott's feeding regime should be radically modified because she is exhibiting food-related aggression. For instance, it is not prudent to continue taking hay or, worse still, concentrate feed into the stable and then appearing to surrender it to her. Instead, food of any description could be introduced into the horse's environment without her seeing it delivered. The feeding site should be moved to break down previous context-specific associations with a certain part of the stable. Use food as a reward only when you are training Mott to recognise vocal praise or neck-scratching as a form of secondary reinforcement. To avoid any tendency to learn to nip at this stage, never offer food rewards by hand.

Secondly, as far as picking up her feet is concerned, I would advise you to retrain Mott from scratch, using a training technique called 'shaping' that relies on teaching the desired behaviour pattern one step at a time. Approach Mott as you would a new foal, and begin by teaching her to tolerate having you groom her legs while her feet remain firmly on the floor. Once she is happy to let you do this, teach her a new verbal command to pick up her feet. Use this command as you encourage her to take the weight off

Offer any food rewards in a bucket.

the leg by gently squeezing the fetlock joint. You will need a friend at her head to offer a reward when Mott has raised her heel off the ground and kept it still for a few seconds. By gradually building on this foundation, you should be able to get her lifting her foot properly within a week.

Finally, we need to get you back in charge when you lead Mott in a head-collar. At her age, she should already have reached the point in her education when she can easily be led around, and certainly be able to be led off the yard on her own. The fact that she is being reared with a donkey rather than with horse company is likely to retard her social development. Although her companion is far better than no animal friend at all, the advantages of her being kept with other horses would be numerous – not the least being that she could play with them more naturally than with a donkey. This would provide an outlet for her boisterousness and her tendency to play-chase – behaviours which, at the moment, are being redirected towards you. If you could move Mott to a yard with several other horses, there would be lots of activity there that could offer her useful learning opportunities. For example, she could be led behind older horses while you are habituating her to traffic, water obstacles and other animals. Meanwhile, in all honesty, the donkey would be better off with a donkey friend of her own. She would rapidly become affiliated with a member of her own species and the bond that developed would be stronger than her current attachment to Mott.

Leading youngstock around with the minimum of fuss should involve the use of consistent vocal stimuli, the manipulation of their innate tendency to follow, and the help of an experienced assistant capable of driving a horse on from behind within seconds of any attempt to baulk. If punishment has to be administered, it should be delivered within two seconds if the horse is to associate it with the unwanted behaviour. The application of discipline in the episode that you have described in your letter involved a considerable delay. This may well have reliably trained Mott to defend herself in such circumstances against any approaches from humans.

Aversion

Aversion, which can be innate or learned, helps animals to avoid unpleasant things in their environment. A natural example would be the way in which a foal learns to avoid hedgehogs because they are painful to touch. Unpleasant experiences acquire a special significance in the memory of prey animals, because they can afford to make so few mistakes in their constant battle to avoid succumbing to predation. (*See also* Memory, p. 55; Learning, p. 52.)

Just as a foal may learn to avoid hedgehogs or thistles, he can develop the same dislike for vets. Naturally enough, vets are not seen by horses as dedicated professionals who have been through five years of study and examinations and beer-drinking for the greater good of Equidae everywhere. On the contrary, they are viewed as the most unpredictable of characters, who arrive unexpectedly on Monday to do nothing more threatening than make a meticulous drawing for legal identification purposes, yet expect you to stand just as still on Tuesday when they insert a needle into your buttocks.

Question
My Welsh cob, Daffyd, is very popular with everyone on our eventing yard. He is very gentle with children and has competed with numerous teenagers, taking them successfully out of pony classes and into open competition. He is excellent in traffic, in the horsebox and in the stable. In fact, the only thing that seems to faze him is our poor vet, who turns him into a gibbering wreck leaping around in all directions. It's not just male handlers that he hates, because he is as good as gold with my husband and the blacksmith. When the vet brought a female student with him on his rounds, Daffyd was just as fearful of her, especially when she tried to inject him. Why is he so quick to change his personality in the presence of a vet, and how can he spot them so easily? Is there any way of improving his behaviour? I'm concerned that one day, in an emergency, he could need a vet to stitch him up but might not allow him near enough to be able to help.

Answer
Vets offer a number of characteristic cues that horses recognise. We are not just talking here about visual markers like overalls, but also smells of substances such as surgical spirit and the lingering scent of fear from previous patients.

There are some horses that cannot be easily approached by vets and, you are quite right, they can be a danger to themselves because they have to be sedated for thorough examination. This use of drugs as a prerequisite for clinical assessment and diagnosis is very unhelpful in life-threatening situations like colic, which require an accurate assessment of the animal's physiological parameters. Your vet will, no doubt, agree that life would be more enjoyable if fewer of his patients were scared of him. Many horse-lovers qualify as horse-doctors every year, only to find to their considerable dismay that their favourite species wants absolutely nothing to do with them!

This negative association with vets is completely understandable because, as far as Daffyd is concerned, they are never paired with positive stimuli. Horses' mistrust of vets is intermittently reinforced with pain and discomfort – for instance, when torn skin is stitched or rectal examinations are conducted. This, together with vets' unpredictable behaviour, makes them particularly difficult to abide, and so horses that develop this sort of phobia are treated in a particular way by most seasoned veterinarians. For instance, when it is time for the annual vaccination, the vet will usually acknowledge that to let the horse see the needle does not actually help him to come to terms with it! So he tends to inject quickly and then rapidly retreat to a safe distance, thus bringing not only fear and pain, but also an unwelcome startle.

If your vet is co-operative, you may be able to persuade him to help in a programme of desensitisation and counter-conditioning. I have used this system many times with my own clients and the results are very encouraging, with most animals becoming easier to examine and – just as important – to treat.

First, you may have to convince the vet of the virtues of getting Daffyd to calm down in his presence. Then, if he wears an overall or clinical examination coat, go out and buy a similar one. Ask him to wear it on his rounds for a while, so that you will be able to use it as a reminder of the visual and olfactory cues that Daffyd associates with your vet. Next, take the overall back and wear it whenever you feed the horse. Make certain that you do not rush him. When you are wearing the overall, let him make any approach towards you. Do not try to calm him down if he acts nervously. Equally, do not leave the stable until he stops leaping around. When he is happy to stand still in the presence of the overall, groom him and pet him as much as possible. Then move on to mimicking injection techniques – without, of course, any needle. Just bounce your clenched fist up and down on his quarters and neck while he eats his evening meal. You should also get him to stand quietly while you 'skin-twitch' his neck – in other words, while you grasp and turn a fold of skin in front of his shoulder.

As with any behaviour modification programme you will know if you are advancing too rapidly because Daffyd's behaviour will become unpredictable, and fear will re-emerge. Remember, don't assume that the programme is not working if his behaviour starts to regress. Instead, take it as a signal to return to the previous stage and re-establish good behaviour with those stimuli before moving on.

The next step is to ask your husband to carry out the same programme of systematic feeding, grooming and mock treatment. You can join in during the latter stages and offer Daffyd rewards for being calm, because this is the way you will reinforce desirable behaviour when the vet wants to do real injections, stitch-ups and so forth. Above all, do not use food as a bribe to distract him once he has started acting up. The sort of association that this would produce can sometimes encourage the behaviour you are seeking to extinguish.

You will be ready to ask your vet to co-operate once more at the point when Daffyd allows your husband to perform mock injections. The one important step that remains is to introduce some more positive stimuli with the vet himself. All you have to do here is get him to go in and stroke Daffyd whenever he visits the yard. Hopefully, the next time Daffyd requires veterinary treatment will be some way down the track, and this will give you enough time to estab-lish in him a new set of behaviours *vis-à–vis* the veterinary profession.

There are now some rather expensive pressure guns that some vets use routinely to deliver local anaesthesia as part of 'nerve-block' examinations for lameness. I have found these useful for needle-shy horses, because the needle itself can be introduced gently through a blob of local anaesthetic under the skin. The same method can be used to introduce local anaesthetic through a fold of twitched skin, which is why I advocate the inclusion of this procedure in the desensitisation programme.

Finally, on a safety note, never attempt to introduce poten-tially frightening stimuli such as mock injections unless there is a firm layer of bedding on the floor to prevent you or Daffyd from slipping. Similarly, ensure that any water buckets have been removed from the loose-box and that you are not the only person on the yard.

Question

I am having a lot of trouble with my pony, Dennis, because he hates men. My boyfriend really tries very hard to make friends with him, but he is quite nervous and gets scared when Dennis leaps into the corner of the box and then turns on him. Now they just avoid each other. It is a very antisocial situation and it means that my boyfriend and I don't spend our free time together. He just sits in the car and listens to the radio when I'm seeing to Dennis. I know that horses can't be jealous, but is there any other reason for this sort of discrimination?

Answer

Apart from animals in the racing and trotting industries, most horses are exposed to women more than to men. So, because horses prefer familiar companions, broadly speaking they are simply more at home with female handlers. It is also a recognised fact that, in general, men are less affectionate towards animals than women are. This can mean that minor differences, such as the tone of a man's voice, may be less easily associated with affection. From my own observations, it seems that men are generally more likely to hit a horse when they feel that punishment is due. Add to that the fact that the majority of vets are men, and one begins to realise why so many horses have learned to avoid rather than to trust men.

Here is a selection of reasons why Dennis may have reacted with fear the first time your boyfriend entered his stable. Because your boyfriend was nervous as well as unfamiliar to Dennis, the pony's mistrust would have been confirmed. The man suddenly moving out of his way would do nothing to calm the pony primed for action. The body language between the two would have allowed fear to escalate in both parties.

In this sort of case, the most important point to mention to your boyfriend is that, when dealing with Dennis, he should take plenty of time and let the pony do the approaching rather than the other way round. When Dennis jumps into the corner of the stable because he is frightened of the prospect of being caught by a man, he does so because the corner offers sanctuary. This being the case, the worst thing you can do is to invade his safe space and thereby confirm that you are a scary monster from which there is no escape. This is the point at which many horses would defend themselves by turning their quarters on you and offering you both barrels.

If your boyfriend genuinely wants to break down the unwelcome associations that Dennis has for men, he will have to gradually dilute the pony's established responses by a programme of habituation. This means presenting Dennis with the threatening stimulus time and time again, in a non-threatening context, until his response wanes. One tip is to start the programme after a ride so that Dennis is slightly fatigued and tuned in to human instruction. With Dennis in his box, ask your boyfriend to feed him by taking the bucket in and standing quietly with it. But he will need to be very patient, as some horses take ages to convince themselves that they are not contending with a trap.

Avoidance
For creatures of flight, avoidance is the policy usually adopted when frightening stimuli are presented. For feral horses, the avoidance distance in relation to humans is typically more than five metres (fifteen feet), but this is dependent on their prior experience and the humans' behaviour.

In avoidance conditioning the horse learns that, if it responds appropriately to a signal, it will avoid receiving an aversive stimulus that would otherwise occur. Take, for example, the lunging-whip, which can be brought closer to the horse as a signal to increase the forward pace. By responding correctly the horse avoids feeling the whip itself. Although, strictly speaking, avoidance conditioning involves animals avoiding stimuli that they know to be unpleasant, this process can also operate for stimuli that are merely *believed* to be aversive. This means that superstitions can be generated in animals, and these can evoke as much avoidance behaviour as real threats.

Question
We have a family pony called Midda who is about twenty years old. She is completely bomb-proof and has taken all my children in turn to Pony Club camp every year for the last decade. She is a truly 'handy pony' except when it comes to water, which really brings out the stubborn side of her nature. Despite trying everything possible, we cannot persuade her to go anywhere near a puddle while out hacking. The more she is encouraged to approach water on the ground, the more stroppy she gets. Although she is not at

all dangerous when she is being disobedient and although I know that she is too old to change, can you explain why some horses have this tendency to avoid puddles?

Answer
You have described one of the commonest features of horses and ponies that belong to what I call the 'self-preservation society'. These are the equine characters who take virtually no risks in life. Putting it very simply, Midda does not trust what she cannot see. Her feet are extremely important to her, so it makes sense for her to tread carefully on the ground that she can see, rather than risk putting them into water. Regardless of the appearance of the puddle's surface, there is no way Midda can tell what is lurking underneath or, indeed, how deep the puddle is.

This fear of the unknown is innate, but her avoidance is likely to have been reinforced by anyone who has forced her closer and closer to the threat. Ultimately, Midda will have learned that the sight of an approaching puddle means that she is probably about to get kicked and cajoled, as well as threatened with the monsters lurking under the puddle's surface. It is easy to see how the superstitious components of Midda's fear are amplified under these circumstances.

With a youngster that shows Midda's tendency to avoid water, many trainers are prone to reach for whips and ropes to coerce the horse into the threatening abyss. A more humane and effective way to overcome this fear is to use the dam, or an affiliated peer, as a lure. With patience, we can use the horse's innate following response to our advantage. After all, in this way, generations of young feral horses have learned to follow their herd members through all manner of hazards.

B

Bands

Natal bands are the family groups that make up herds of horses. Usually having no more than ten members, bands are matriarchies, with the several higher-ranking females often being good friends or affiliates. Band size, and cohesion within a band, seem to be important factors in its breeding success, with the lowest foaling and foal survival rates being found in smaller and unstable bands.

One of the most important factors affecting the stability of the herd is the number of stallions around. Too many stray stallions can cause a constant flux with continual leadership challenges, while too few males in the vicinity means that bands do not remain cohesive groups and so may disperse. On rare occasions there are reports of two stallions, a dominant and a subordinate, that co-operate in the defence of a harem. These harems are larger and more stable than most, with the breeding rights being inherited by the henchman, should the boss disappear for whatever reason.

Dispersal is a normal stage in the maternal band's social organisation, and is an important means of reducing the chances of inbreeding. With the departure of juvenile horses, their genes spread to new habitats and the possibility of their mating with one of their parents is minimised. This appears to be more important for males than for females, because the stallion within each harem regularly changes while the mares are what makes the band such a cohesive unit. The cohesion may, however, be jeopardised by the death or removal of a key member of the harem. If a split of this sort occurs. the resulting subgroups may then join other bands.

Barging
In horses, the head, shoulder and thigh tend to be used to push other animals, while the chest is most often used to move barriers.

Barging can be used to confirm dominance in horses of established rank, although it is more likely to arise from fear in the first instance. Horses that barge through doorways have often been trained to race on the flat – that is, with the use of starting-stalls, which can prove perpetually aversive to them. And things become so much worse when barging leads to a battle between handler and horse. The horse rapidly perceives the mounting stress which passage through doorways provokes, and as a result he becomes more tense. The fact that his head is held so very tightly to prevent him carting his handler through the doorway or, worse still, crushing him, serves only to reinforce his anxiety.

Question
I have a thirteen-year-old Thoroughbred brood mare, Agnes, whom I bought as a racing reject nine years ago. She is generally very quiet and doesn't get worked up about being left in her stable or being transported to and from the stud. The stud grooms always seem very happy to have her back at the stud, but she does tend to come home with terrible scars because she doesn't hold her own in equine company. The scars, however, are not all from other horses, because she self-inflicts an awful lot of damage by rushing in and out of the loose-box twice a day. She is usually stabled at the stud, either because she has a foal at foot or because she is being kept under bright lights to bring her into season early. I tend to keep her at grass and so have very few problems, but on the odd occasion that I do bring her in, she tends to rush through the doorway into the box and gets terribly panic-stricken if I restrain her. Why do horses behave in this way?

Answer
This is a learned behaviour that often has its origins in flat-racing, which requires a horse to learn how to race from starting-stalls. What tends to happen is that being taken through narrow openings becomes an issue with the animal. Other causes include any accident that has beset her while

being taken through a doorway – for instance, if she has not been led through at right angles to the aperture and has knocked her hip as a result. Much of the rushing behaviour comes from a fear of being trapped, and so any subsequent ill-judged barging that leads to hip injuries only serves to confirm to the horse that she was right to worry about not getting through the doorway unharmed. In this way, the gravity of the phobia and the expression of the fear tend to spiral.

The reward from this behaviour comes from getting to the other side of a perceived trap. For instance, getting into a box can be rewarding, because there may be food waiting there and, once the horse is on the other side of it, her anxiety about being trapped by the doorway will subside. Getting out of the box can be rewarding too because it usually heralds being turned out, and again it can remove the threat that the doorway represents.

Regardless of how Agnes developed her fear in the first place, your only strategy can be to habituate her to the stimuli that she fears. Any programme to modify such an established behaviour will take a great deal of time and effort. For this reason, you can hardly ask the stud to conduct a programme, and so you will have to do it yourself. What you need to do is to change her management at home so that she is exposed to the fear-eliciting stimuli without them threatening her. The programme can be tackled in two phases: the first, to address the fear of the sight of the doorway; and the second, to address the fear of being led through it.

Firstly, build a temporary pen adjoining her box (using sheep hurdles, for instance), cushion the sides of the stable door jambs (old blankets are ideal for this job), then simply let her come and go in and out of the box as she pleases. Alternate the location of any hay nets and feed tubs that are left with her so that she has to move in and out several times a day. Without the pressure of you or a groom having to position her for her rush through the doorway, Agnes will learn that she can control her own progress and take her time over this threatening manoeuvre. After two or three weeks under this regime, most horses have lost their need to rush and barge through doorways.

The next step is to ensure that Agnes can maintain her

new composure in the presence of a human. To do this, keep the pen in place and spend time with her over the following week leading her to, but not through, the doorway. The aim here is to break down the anticipation component of the unwelcome behaviour. When you are happy that there is no panic involved with your doing this from either side of the doorway, you can start to lead Agnes in and out. Ultimately, you should aim to get her standing in the doorway to be stroked and fed. The removal of the cushions and the pen marks the final step, which normally provokes little regression. Beyond this point, most horses can be treated as normal.

Biting

Question
Ever since I bought my Irish draught mare, Bridie, as a four-year-old she has turned to bite when I tighten up her girth. She doesn't resent me putting the saddle on, but as soon as I lift the saddle flap she starts glaring at me and tossing her head towards me in a threatening fashion. She does the same thing when I tighten the surcingle of her rug. I never hurt her, so why does she do this? What can I do to improve the situation?

Answer
This is a learned behaviour that takes a very long time to become extinguished. The development of this response involves past or current pain – in other words, punishment. Furthermore, because this punishment is intermittent the response becomes thoroughly ingrained on the horse's memory. Although it is not a matter of urgency, I would encourage you to ask your veterinary surgeon to examine your mare's back next time he is in the area. This is just to ensure that no ongoing disease or injury is causing the behaviour. For the same reason, check that your saddle is well fitted, and remember to use it with a numnah (saddle pad) to minimise the chill it brings to the skin of the back when the girth is tightened.

Assuming that your mare and her saddle are given the all-clear, you can concentrate on changing her response to the girthing procedure. You have to be able to devote time to this programme and to accept that tacking up will be a protracted business for the next couple of months. This is because the only way to break down the association with pain is to present the stimulus without actually tightening the girth at all. You may be tightening her girth in three or four steps already, but now is the time to double that figure so that the girth-tightening process becomes extremely gradual. You should also be doing all this well in advance of any ridden work. This will curb your enthusiasm to get the girth tight in order to start the ride. It will also mean that, assuming that she is not aggressive around food, Bridie can be fed while the girth is being dealt with. This is useful, since it both distracts her and makes biting less likely because the motivation to feed tends to outweigh the motivation to bite.

I recommend that you invest in an elasticated girth, a sheepskin girth-guard and a mounting-block. All of these pieces of equipment help to make the girthing business less painful. The elastic allows a gradation between holes on the girth straps and means that your mare will not have to anticipate the increase of girth pressure in a notchwise fashion. Similarly, the girth-guard helps by cushioning the edges of the girth and minimising any possible pinching effect. With a mounting-block, you never need to have the girth at its tightest before you mount, and it also reduces the twisting effect that mounting generally tends to create. All of these things in combination help to reduce the horse's fear of being girthed.

In some respects you are fortunate, because some horses experience both saddles and rugs as cues to imminent pain and discomfort. Understandably, they try to avoid the possibility of unpleasant stimuli by running forward or dodging sideways. When prospective purchasers go to see them in response to an advertisement, these are the horses that are always tacked up before they arrive! It always pays to see and feel a horse's back before he is tacked up – you could thereby save yourself the price of a pre-purchase veterinary examination.

Your horse may simply enjoy travelling at speed.

Bolting

Question
My old cob recently went into a very well earned retirement,
so I set about trying to find a replacement for him. About
a month ago I agreed to have a ten-year-old ex-point-to-
pointer, Quixote, on permanent loan. He is a very elegant
animal but is taking a while to calm down whenever I hack
out on him. Every time I take him on to the moors at the
back of our house he gets terribly fresh and starts leaping
up and down. If I let him trot he soon turns it into a canter,
swiftly followed by a gallop, and that's when I start to lose
control and Quixote starts to bolt. Although he sometimes
terrifies me with this habit I would like to persist with him.
What approach would you suggest?

Answer
Strictly speaking, Quixote is not bolting. Bolting implies
that he is fleeing from something that has frightened him.
Classically, the image of a bolting horse is one in harness
that has been scared by a loud noise behind it and so takes
off. Wearing blinkers and hearing the sound of a clattering
cart that is only designed for movement at trotting speed,
the horse immediately resorts to blind panic and does the
only thing he has evolved to do in red-alert situations –
run. As with red-alert situations in feral horses, the escape
procedure only begins to wind down when the horse realises
that other horses around him are beginning to slow down

(not something that is made any the easier by wearing blinkers) or when he becomes exhausted.

Your horse may simply enjoy travelling at speed. Therefore, rather than bolting, he is simply running away with you. Obviously, my giving this behaviour a different label does not make it any less frightening for you! Perhaps we should consider where this exuberance is coming from. Quixote's breed has been selected for racing, not for hacking. Before ever being galloped, young racehorses are fittened on the roads and they soon learn to associate tarmac with walking and trotting, while grass is the clue that faster gaits are expected.

If you are considering a stronger, that is to say, more severe, bit be prepared to be very careful when applying it. If you do not have good hands, you will end up making matters worse by effectively numbing any sensitivity that remains in his mouth.

You say that you have yet to canter Quixote without losing control. So it sounds to me as though you would both benefit from the opportunity to get to know each other in a safer environment. I would recommend that you hire your nearest manège for an hour and find out what brakes your new horse has. This will allow him to begin to dissociate cantering from galloping and give you back some confidence. If you can't find a schooling area close enough, a small field (with very high hedges!) will work as well, providing the ground is not slippery. Another way of reintroducing him to more civilised paces if you live in a hilly district, may be to ride out in steady company. Only go into a trot after about an hour on the road, when you find a good long downhill stretch. When you arrive at the start of a canter track get your companion to walk around with you in large circles, making sure you ask him for impulsion when he is looking away from the gallop. Remember – you're simply trying to remind him that he has to respond to you. When you are ready, let him go, and use your legs. When he begins to flag use them once more, before actively asking him to pull up. By using the hill, and gravity, in this way you will re-educate him to respond.

Box-walking

You are left in little doubt if the horse that you have just bought is a box-walker. The churning of the entire bed into a track around the box is the classic sign that he has spent the night endlessly retracing his steps. The other striking consequence of this behaviour is fatigue in the perpetrator, who often ends up completely exhausted and covered in a proper 'muck sweat'. The effort that some horses put into it speaks of their motivation to move and their frustration at being confined. Some Thoroughbred youngsters in training use up so much energy in this activity that they cannot be trained; these are the unfortunates that no trainer wants to waste time on. The behaviour has to be declared at public auction and can therefore be a reason for a horse going directly from a bloodstock sale to an abattoir.

The severity of the behaviour varies, with some owners reporting that their horse's box-walking is confined to periods of excitement, while others specify that it is related to the absence or departure of other horses. Similarly, some box-walkers do it only in anticipation of work – for instance, on the morning of a hunt – while others do it only when they are out of work, in season or without company. A very successful endurance rider once told me that a horse she owned would box-walk all night, and complete forty miles with a normal pulse the following day, then go on to box-walk all of the following night. Interestingly, of all the equestrian disciplines endurance riding is dogged by very few stereotypies, but of the behaviours that do arise box-walking is surprisingly prevalent. It is not clear why this should be, although it has been suggested that, as the marathon runners of the horse world, these horses may have discovered their own way of generating a 'jogger's high'. According to human studies, this phenomenon is thought to occur when exhaustion elicits a burst of endorphin production. If horses get this feeling when they run as part of their ridden work, they may actively seek it when they are confined to their boxes.

Although stereotypies often exist independently of their initiating causes, and so can persist despite improvements in the horse's environment, there are reports of some stopping box-walking within a few days of arriving on a new yard. More research is needed to determine how these resolutions come about. In general, older horses do seem to put less effort into this activity than when they were young, but the change is often merely in keeping with a general decline in activity.

Question
We have a Thoroughbred riding pony called Geronimo that box-walks. He does this when he's plaited up and also when he wants to go out to the paddock, but not at night when he comes in to go to bed! He doesn't do it when he has to stay in because of bad weather. It is almost as if he can tell whether it is worth being turned out, and tailors his behaviour accordingly. I've heard of some horses being put to sleep for this activity, but I really don't find it that much of a problem. In fact, I use it as a measure of how well he is feeling, and as his way of telling me what he wants. What I would like to know is why some horses box-walk and others do not.

Answer
The cause of this stereotypic behaviour is described as 'multifactorial' in other words, it takes a combination of factors to create it. Research has shown that there is a hereditary component to it, in that certain Thoroughbred families exhibit more of the behaviour. In addition, weaning methods and current levels of confinement are thought to play a part in the process that turns a normal horse, with genetic tendencies, into a full-blown box-walker.

Attempts to make box-walking more difficult for the horse, such as putting bales and tyres on the floor of the box, only ever seem to make its frustration more acute. Such techniques should be avoided in favour of increased access to placid companions and exercise facilities. There are some severely affected horses that do this route-tracing exclusively in one direction, to the extent that muscles build up on one side of the back while wasting on the other. These animals are actually indulging in a form of self-mutilation and, whenever possible, should be turned out permanently on humane grounds.

Bucking

Question
I have recently bought a five-year-old Cleveland Bay × Thoroughbred gelding called Captain that I intend to take hunting next season. He is settling in very well and seems to enjoy being ridden, although we are doing only light

work at present. The only nagging problem I have with him is that he bucks every time I ask him to canter. Why should he do this?

Answer
Essentially, bucking happens in feral horse behaviour either as an attempt to get rid of a predator or as part of play. In your case, it sounds very much as though Captain is a healthy young horse with a taste for a bit of fun. If there were any malice, I'm sure he would have succeeded in getting rid of you by now; but all the same I recognise that it is not the most polite form of behaviour! Although the bucks may become less frequent when he goes into more serious work, I would urge you to have your saddle checked before you do much more, because an ill-fitting piece of tack can often cause a twinge or two of pain when its wearer is asked to move up a pace.

Some horses develop a habit of bucking as a kind of punctuation to mark the end of trotting and the start of the day's first canter. To avoid the risk of coming off this sort of animal, some owners with the problem tend to lunge their horses before riding them, but this doesn't help when one is trying to bring a horse into work gradually and trying to prevent him careering around on a lungeline. The other way to avoid trouble when riding your gelding is simply to ask for a few canter strides at some point before resuming a trot, while keeping a sensitive contact on his mouth. The prerequisite for any buck is that the horse be able to get his head down. If you can be sensitive enough with your hands to detect your horse's attempt to increase the length of the reins, you should be able to nip any acrobatics display in the bud.

C

Castration

The decision on whether to castrate usually depends on the value of any potential stud fee. Most people in the UK estimate the benefits of a colt's future earnings to be unlikely to outweigh the inconvenience of having an entire male around. The Continental systems of horse husbandry are far more prepared to embrace the management of large numbers of stallions. This cultural difference, and the increased selection it offers, may be one of the reasons for the current success that warm-bloods are enjoying worldwide as performance animals.

The main decision that we are left to puzzle over is *when* to castrate. The longer the operation is postponed, the more mature the colt's crest will become, but there are very few other advantages to keeping him entire once the decision to 'cut' has been made. If he can be turned out in an unpoached paddock after surgery, this will be very useful in reducing the swelling that will appear in his scrotum. Therefore, most colt owners aim to have their foals castrated when the weather is mild but the flies are not at their worst.

The period of retained sexual desire depends on the age and experience of the stallion when he is castrated. Most adult stallions will still demonstrate sexual desire for at least a year after surgery.

Catching

Question
Our family owns a Welsh cob called Jetson, who really loves his food and never seems to lose condition whatever the time of year. He is a real tank, and can be quite difficult to stop once he gets going in open country. As far as perform-

ance goes, he is an ideal family pony, but when it comes to being caught he is an absolute pain. He always gives us the run-around and canters away for ten minutes or so before he lets us walk up to him and catch him. I have noticed that he takes longer to catch in the summer months. Can you suggest why this should be?

Answer
The horses that eventually do allow themselves to be caught are not frightened of being handled – they would just rather be left to their own devices. In the summer months, many of these characters view the daily arrival of their owners as the end of their opportunity to munch the grass. They are taken away from their companions and led into a stable or tied up in a yard where food is unavailable. Then they are groomed and tacked up. And the reward for co-operating with this process is minimal.

During the summer, horses are usually brought in from the paddock just for exercise. Any food they may receive is given after work, often just before being turned out again, because at that point it is processed better by the digestive tract. During the winter, we have all seen horses waiting to come in at night; this is in anticipation of food, not because they want to have four walls around them. The abundance of food in the summer months also means that the typical horse's motivation to get a food reward is reduced. In Jetson's case, with his ample girth, I would recommend sectioning off part of the field with electric fencing. This helps in two ways: by reducing the space he has available to run around in, and by limiting the food available so that he is more motivated to come up to you for a reward.

This is why giving a tiny token feed from a bucket is a good habit to get into, even in summer when many horses can be worked on grass alone. I say 'tiny' and 'token' because it is important to emphasise at this point that over-feeding is far more common than underfeeding. I feel that far more work can be asked of horses at grass than is currently the norm. Small rewards are also best because they can be hidden in a pocket and given only when the pony has been caught. Taking a bucket into a field is a useful bribe, but many ponies grow to regard this visual and auditory cue as a prerequisite to being caught. These are the

... horses quickly get used to the presence of a short
trailing line while grazing.

ones that show their true colours when you attempt to catch
them *without* a bucket.

Catching can be made easier by the use of a short length
of baling-twine attached to the central D-ring of the head-
collar. Horses quickly get used to the presence of a short,
trailing line while grazing. It should have no knots or loops
in it, so that should either of the front feet tread on it, the
horse can easily release his head by tugging the twine from
under the hoof.

Question
My Welsh Section C pony, Samuel, has never been very
friendly to me or my parents, but that has always been OK
because he is such a good jumping pony that his talent
makes up for things. We recently moved house, however, so
Samuel changed fields, and he has become very vicious in

his paddock. He runs at me when I go to catch him and tries to bite me. My mum has to catch him for me now and she says that we might sell him because he isn't quite as good at jumping as he used to be. Why do ponies suddenly start getting angry about being caught?

Answer
It sounds very much as though something has changed in Samuel's life to cause this behaviour change. Being moved to a different field could be the cause if he has bonded with a horse in the new paddock and realises that your arrival signals a period of separation from his friend. Try to see who his closest friend is, and take some time to record how he behaves when other horses come between him and his buddy. Although horses rarely become so very strongly bonded that they respond violently to separation, the problem has occasionally been identified as a cause of aggression.

The other possibility is that it is because he is becoming stale that Samuel has developed an unpleasant association with being caught. This would tie in with your comment about him being less of a show-jumping star than he used to be. It would be worth asking your veterinary surgeon to examine his back to check that pain is not at the root of this reluctance to perform. Horses in pain can become unpredictable, and it's important to eliminate this before continuing to ask him to jump.

With any horse that is becoming aggressive in the field, it is imperative that you take no chances. So, use the usual safety gear: wear boots, gloves and skullcap, not least for personal protection but also to boost your confidence, which often suffers considerably in these situations. Instead of going up to Samuel directly and running the risk of him seeing you as a threat, I recommend that you concentrate on another horse in the field, preferably one subordinate to Samuel. Train this stooge to run up to you for a food reward whenever you enter the field (this is incredibly easy if you are consistent and timely with your rewards). You will find that Samuel begins to show interest in you as a source of benevolence, rather than viewing you as a threat. Until he is approaching you with his ears forward, show no interest in him. When this does happen, throw him a snack and then withdraw for the day. Aim to reshape his behaviour over two or three weeks, during which time you need to break from your catching-riding routine to allow him to concentrate on learning a new set of field manners.

Clipping

Question
Marshy, my part-bred Arab mare, has always been a rather emotional creature and is very sensitive to heavy traffic and the sound of gunshot, but her greatest fear is of being clipped. Every time the clippers are switched on she gets panicky, and when they actually come near her she starts trying to climb the walls of the box. I usually get the vet to sedate her to be clipped, but this is far from ideal. I'm embarrassed to say that all the horses I have ever owned have been the same. I realise that horses are not supposed to lose their coats in the winter, but this cannot be the reason for so many of them resenting the procedure! Do you have any advice on reducing the stress both Marshy and I suffer when it is time for a haircut?

Answer
Clipping can be made easier by ensuring, firstly, that the horse is clean and dry; and secondly, that the clippers are regularly serviced and are powerful enough for the job in hand. Cool clippers are less likely to alarm the horse than warm ones, which are also likely to pull hairs by jamming. For horses, clipping can never be pleasant because it brings with it unusual noise, heat and vibration as well as the possibility of occasionally being nicked. Given that you are content with the state of your clippers, there are a few steps you can take to condition a new response to the threat that clippers represent for your horse. Your reluctance to rely on chemical sedation is justified from the point of view both of expense and of Marshy's continuing education. Horses under sedation cannot learn, so no matter how placidly you clip her once she is sedated she will not become habituated to the aversive stimuli. The other problem with chemical sedation is that occasionally, as a side-effect, it can cause sweating, and that makes clipping very difficult.

For these reasons I recommend that, before next season's clipping begins, you use the following tried and tested counter-conditioning programme to modify Marshy's response. All you have to do is switch on a pair of clippers outside her box before every feeding time. Before long, she will reliably associate the sound with something pleasant. Once this association is established, get to work on the other challenging characteristics of clippers – their tendency to vibrate and become warm. Again, use these clipping features to announce the arrival of food. In scientifically controlled tests, the use of food has been proved to develop new responses to clipping stimuli. This technique fails only in horses that have been rushed through a programme too quickly before being clipped, or in those that remember pain at the time of clipping.

Finally, since you mention that all of your horses have been the same as far as clipping is concerned, consider the possibility that you are inadvertently reinforcing the unwelcome behaviour. It is quite possible that you have built up an anxious approach to the whole notion of clipping. This anxiety would be readily transmitted to any animal, but especially to your own horse, who spots the difference between your hyped-up state and your usual self. Being social animals, horses are very sensitive to the behavioural and odour changes that signify stress, and Marshy will by now have taught herself that your state of readiness for the Battle of the Clippers should alert her to panic. If this is the case, ask someone else to start the clipping next time Marshy-with-her-new-associations needs a haircut. You can take over once she has shown that she really is settled.

Companions

The way horses organise themselves socially is rather intriguing. Bonds appear between members of a stable group, so that much of each day at grass is spent with chosen companions. It is probably because 'friendship' is the wrong word to describe what is going on that equine friendships seem curious to human observers. For instance, antagonistic interactions are more common between affiliated horses, but these exchanges are less aggressive than with less bonded individuals. Coalitions form between pairs and threesomes which help the members of the coalitions to defend resources such as food. This is perhaps most obvious when a group of horses are given hay out in the paddock.

Mother and daughter associations have been found to be much more long-term than those between a dam and her male offspring. Stable bonds are also found in the breeding relationship between a stallion and the mares in his harem. In feral situations the average period of harem ownership is four years, and during this time mutual grooming and sexual interactions seem to consolidate the bond between them. While a stallion typically guards the integrity of his group, mares often demonstrate a mutual attachment to their stallion by soliciting his company exclusively when they are sexually receptive and waiting for him when he has been detained for whatever reason.

Coprophagia

The equine snack-habits that prompt a steady stream of correspondence involve those horses that elect to eat droppings. In foals this behaviour is to be expected, since it is a completely normal part of the repertoire that allows young horses to populate their large bowels with the organisms responsible for digestion, and it also supplies them with cholates, which are necessary for the development of a healthy nervous system. If mares and foals are wormed regularly, dung consumption does not increase parasite populations, but it can cause gastrointestinal upsets through the transmission of bacterial pathogens.

The other horses that are seen eating their own droppings are those that are forced to exist on low-roughage diets. Even though such diets provide adequate amounts of the bare necessities, they do not do so in a way that meets a horse's innate need for a lengthy foraging period. The result is that he finishes his meal swiftly and then is left to search through his bedding for anything remotely edible. This searching and sifting process occupies so much of the horse's time that he effectively blends the bedding with the faeces. In this way, as he forages, he is constantly presented with fragments of his own faecal output. He then rapidly loses his innate aversion to this commodity – if he didn't, he would not be able to satisfy his inborn motivation to spend most of the day searching for food. In the short term, the habit can become so ingrained that I have seen fat horses that have been kept on complete diets for an extended period turn round and tuck into fresh piles of their own faeces even when turned out at grass. However, once owners have corrected dietary shortcomings, they always report the eventual disapearance of this behaviour.

Crib-biting and wind-sucking

Caged tigers that repeatedly pace up and down their enclosures raise public concern about welfare in zoos. On a less exotic scale, similar behaviours are seen in horses and ponies throughout the country. Known in horse lore as 'stable vices' and saddled with descriptive labels such as box-walking, weaving, wind-sucking and crib-biting, these behaviours tend to cause more embarrassment than concern. Despite this, questions regarding 'stereotypies', as these activities are more correctly described, have been fielded by behaviourists and vets for decades. I have recently been fortunate enough to receive funding to find some answers, and I outline here the way I went about my research.

My first step was to develop an understanding of equine stereotypies by surveying a large group of Thoroughbred racehorses. Results involving 4,468 horses in training showed the prevalence of stereotypies to be 11 per cent. Statistical analysis identified a number of husbandry factors that were associated with peaks in prevalence, including the amount and variety of the forage, as well as the type of bedding (either straw or less edible alternatives) that the horses are given. This seems to underline the importance of foraging in equids, which devote up to sixteen hours a day to it in the feral state, whereas stabled horses, given concentrated feedstuffs, may finish their daily ration in less than three hours. And it appears that while some attempt to eat their beds, others develop stereotypies. While stereotypies have never been recorded in feral animals, some domesticated bloodlines seem especially prone to these behavioural abnormalities; and this illustrates the other factor involved in the appearance of stereotypies – heredity. Occasionally, we receive reports of foals that develop anomalous behaviour patterns before they experience intensive management. For example, they can start crib-biting from the age of two months, regardless of whether their mother or any field-mates are doing the same.

The stereotypy that trainers found most frustrating was

crib-biting, which was reported in 5.5 per cent of the racing Thoroughbred population. A crib-biter holds on to a fixed object with its incisors and pulls back, often emitting a characteristic grunt thought to signify the swallowing of air. This was the behaviour I decided to concentrate on, because it can be manipulated experimentally and because it has traditionally been linked to various forms of ill-health. For instance, in 1912 Captain H. S. Mosley wrote that crib-biting was 'a psychopathological condition . . . closely associated with the sexual organs' and 'a form of mental masturbation'. These days, it is not so much imagined moral deficits as the physical consequences of crib-biting such as tooth-wear and an increased susceptibility to colic that prompt owners to attempt prevention via tight collars or even surgery. Wind-sucking is said to occur when a horse accomplishes the grunting noise without having to hold on to a fixed object. Sometimes this extra trick results from attempts to prevent the grasping component of crib-biting with aversion therapy, for instance by putting electric-fencing wire on all ledges.

To determine the origin of the grunting noise, eight obliging crib-biters were X-rayed while producing it (with some horses crib-biting seven thousand times a day, the radiographers didn't have long to wait!). What we saw did nothing to support the view that air was actively ingested, because there was no movement of the tongue as one would expect in true swallowing. Instead, each horse showed an explosive distension of the oesophagus which prompted no peristalsis. The grunt was generated by the soft palate flapping as air rushed from the mouth on its way to the oesophagus.

Having established the prevalence, the risk factors and the morphology of crib-biting, I wanted to know why horses do it. I was able to show that those that were prevented from crib-biting by wearing a collar for twenty-four hours performed more of the stereotypy than they had before their day of abstinence. Reminiscent of a smoker disembarking from a Virgin Atlantic flight and then bingeing, this rebound effect suggested an internal motivation or even an addiction to crib-biting. It may also account for reports of horses that are required to wear collars becoming bad-tempered! Furthermore, it may explain why surgical procedures to 'cure' crib-biting have such variable success rates. The crib-biter's motivation to perform the behaviour remains high even when his ability to do so is compromised by the discomfort or deformation that follows surgery.

It seemed likely that a stress response would accompany such a period of deprivation, especially since people have suggested that stereotypies enable animals to become 'spaced out' on endorphins (the body's own equivalent of morphine) in order to cope with unacceptable environments. So we recruited more horses to test the theory and to compare the short-term deprivation of crib-biting with the temporary withdrawal of another activity that is important to horses – eating.

With the help of a patient carpenter and several resourceful crib-biters who identified the tiniest of lumps, lips and ledges, we built six projection-free stables. Using these, we could prevent crib-biting for extended periods while taking hourly blood samples. Intriguingly, deprivation of neither crib-biting alone nor food alone created a stress response. However, when the horses were deprived of both food *and* the opportunity to crib-bite, they showed a dramatic rise in the plasma stress response. This finding exposed the link between foraging and crib-biting and explains why restricted feeding is a management factor associated with an increase in abnormal behaviour in racehorses. Additionally, we found that crib-biters ate more than normal horses when they were unable to crib-bite. This underlines the fact that affected horses have greater oral needs than their normal counterparts.

With the Bristol team I have shown that crib-biting, far from being a form of misbehaviour, is an elaborate technique that some horses use to offset the inadequacies of a concentrated diet. However, once established, the behaviour is virtually incurable since it is intrinsically rewarding and so comes to exist independently of its initiating causes. It seems that crib-biters are better off (provided their inherent tendency to develop colic is low) being allowed to crib-bite, but on cushioned surfaces that minimise the risk of incisor erosion.

Question

I read about your work with equine stereotypies and was wondering whether you could help me with a two-year-old seven-eighths bred filly that I have just bought. She comes from very good eventing and racing bloodlines, and I have paid a small fortune for her with advanced eventing in mind. She has been well handled and is very sweet in the box, but has a tendency to seize hold of the top of the stable door between mouthfuls of food. As you have probably guessed, I am concerned that she is about to start crib-biting. It is only hearsay, but I am told that her sire was a wind-sucker. What do you think I should do? I have owned her for four weeks now – is it too late to claim against the vendors for not declaring this behaviour trait?

Answer

I'm afraid to say that your fears are well founded because wind-sucking and crib-biting are related behaviours that have been shown to be especially prevalent in some Thoroughbred families. In your filly's case, it would appear that she is undergoing a *gradual* change from being normal to being a crib-biter. This is the more common history, and helps to explain why people think that wood-chewing leads to crib-biting: the generalised grabbing of fence rails as a preliminary to pulling back and performing a full-blown crib-bite is misread as destructive chewing.

Cures are rare, but even at this early stage they are still worth attempting. So as a remedial step, I recommend turning her out for the next two years with horses of her own age and with an absolute minimum of concentrate feed. To mature properly, alfalfa and vitamin/mineral supplements are all that she needs in addition to the grass. As I say, it may not effect a permanent cure, but this approach is sure to halt the immediate progress of the developing behaviour pattern. It will at least allow her nervous and digestive systems to mature in as natural a way as possible before intensive management is resumed at four years of age and she becomes a real hot-house flower.

Unfortunately, I suspect that you have no claim against the vendors of this filly. Indeed, in a court of law it is often argued that stereotypies can develop within hours of a horse being placed under a new husbandry system and this is sufficient to convince the court that the animal can be free of any indication of stereotypies one day and begin to crib-bite the next. In my opinion, this area of behavioural development needs further scientific study before pronouncements can be made with confidence.

D

Death

In free-ranging horse groups, death often occurs around water sources. This is something of a puzzle to pathologists, but it seems likely that there are behavioural reasons for a dying animal to seek out water as a last-ditch attempt to survive. In most instances of organ failure a kind of shock develops which involves loss of blood pressure. Since thirst is related to the need to maintain blood volume and hence blood pressure, it may be that drinking is the only appropriate response available in the behavioural repertoire of the moribund horse.

Although the demise of a key herd member has occasionally been cited as the reason for the break-up of a group of feral horses, the death of a single individual does not usually alter the dominance relationship of those that remain. Usually far more profound is the effect of the death on the humans in the departed horse's world. These days the status of horses as companions rather than as working animals leads to many remaining with their owners to enjoy a well deserved retirement when they can no longer be ridden. The decision to request euthanasia for such an animal, for instance when it develops chronic pain, is often harder than if it has to be destroyed in an emergency. Fate seems to give the horse an unhappy knack of displaying heroic bursts of energy on the morning of its planned demise. It is at this time that the owner has to remember that it is his or her responsibility to act on the horse's behalf rather than on sentiment.

The options available to horse owners faced with this painful decision are no longer limited to death by bullet; the use of potent anaesthetic agents and sedatives is becoming more commonplace. Some owners believe, and I am inclined to agree, that it is better to pay the extra expense and be more composed at the time of a companion animal's death than to endure a traumatic farewell that tarnishes one's memory and, possibly, even upsets the horse itself. The price one pays for electing to use drugs rather than a bullet is that the remains of an animal that has died through lethal injection are not suitable for further processing. The traditional final destination of most hunters was at the hunt kennels, but these days the declining popularity of fox-hunting means that many horse owners are not disposed to this option. Furthermore, some owners cannot come to terms with the notion that their beloved horse or pony should be eaten by dogs, regardless of whether they hunt foxes for a living. Any form of 'reclamation' is distasteful to them, and so they have the remains buried or cremated, both of which are expensive ventures.

Defence

Defence in equine communities tends to involve defence of the integrity of the band, since mixing is a threat to it and especially to its harem stallion. The defence of current resources takes second place to defence of the zone around the harem. A space of more than fifty metres (yards) is usually found between the harem of one band of feral horses and the next, but the distance seems to depend largely on the concentration of resources. Therefore, when a band uses a key shared resource such as a watering-hole, the appearance of a second band excites defence of the group rather than of the water.

Defence may also include the defence of personal space, because horses tolerate only certain herd members within a distance of 1.5 metres (five feet). Those allowed closer are either bonded affiliates that offer mutual grooming or, in the case of mares, nursing infants.

Question

My Thoroughbred brood mare, Maisie, has always been very good to work with in the stable, but she seems to be getting more and more protective of her foals as the years go by. I have to take a whip into the box if I go in when she has a foal at foot. She lunges at me and tries to bite when I reach to grab her head-collar. Why does she do this when she knows that I am not a threat?

Answer

It is not uncommon for a mare's protectiveness to increase after the first few foalings, but this trend usually plateaus after three or four. There is nothing that can be done to prevent this defence mechanism, since it is perfectly natural for a mare to develop a space around the mother-infant bond. In feral horses, which spend all their time in one another's company, the business of defending a foal often involves mares threatening prenatal females. So if a mare's defence of her foal can cause the disruption of established affiliations within a herd, it is not surprising that a human like yourself, who pays frequent visits to the group but does not live with them, should be excluded.

With any horse that lunges towards you in the box, you will do better to catch it with a walking-stick than with a whip. Whips can escalate fear in alarmed horses while a walking-stick, once its hook is around a strap on the head-collar, can be used to lead the threatening horse at a safe distance.

Diet

Archaeology tells us a great deal about the development of the modern horse's dentition and the foods that it has evolved to exploit. Furthermore, our knowledge of digestion suggests that of all grazing herbivores the horse as a hind-gut fermenter is best adapted to tackle grasses that offer a low-protein but high-fibre content.

The way horses select their food when they are free-ranging depends on what is available. They certainly exhibit preferences, and when able to forage at liberty can readily locate the best pickings. The availability of food follows seasonal changes, and this can have effects on the cyclicity of mares over and above changes in daylight length. These nutritional factors can also influence the length of gestation, with well fed mares appearing to foal slightly earlier than mares on more meagre rations. These are just two ways in which evolution has favoured those horses that maximise their reproductive success by being selective grazers. Since animals seem to have little sense of planning, they usually focus exclusively on a given food source for as long as it is around. This helps them to make the most of transiently available forage, but has the disadvantage of making gorging possible.

Question

Last summer, the ponies and cobs that I looked after were kept in the fairly rough outskirts of town. The local children were adept at firemongering, and during the summer months the lighting of grass fires seemed to be a source of particular joy to them. My greatest fear was that one day they would select our rented paddock as a suitable venue for one of their pyrotechnic conventions. They had already burned several acres of adjoining marshland and seemed to be running short of space.

My fears turned out to be misplaced rather than ill-founded – the local 'youth group' decided to pull the fence down instead of burning the grass. This meant that the herd spilled out on to the marsh, which was enjoying a spurt of regrowth after the latest fire. The horses could not believe their luck and spent the whole day munching until I was able to gather them together after school. When I reached them, Nessie, the bossiest and greediest mare in the group, was unable to move without staggering around in an alarming fashion. When the vet arrived, he said she had induced acute laminitis by consuming too much readily available carbohydrate. It was the grazing equivalent of breaking into the feed shed, something Nessie would have done with equal relish.

Basically, my question is this: Why did she not stop eating when she had had enough?

Answer

First of all, may I say how relieved I am that you are no longer in the dreadful situation you describe. I do hope that you have found somewhere less prone to outside interference. Keeping horses in built-up areas can be a complete nightmare. The plight of the inner-city horse and pony is a cause of concern to many veterinarians and welfare groups, and not simply because of the over-grazing to which paddocks are subjected. The instances of cruelty to these horses are appalling, with reports of attacks by knives, dogs and fireworks being far from uncommon.

You were quite right to regard Nessie's symptoms as very serious. Your vet certainly had his eyes open too, and no doubt treated the laminitis promptly and aggressively to avoid any long-term damage to her feet. This is one of the best illustrations I have come across of the fact that giving animals a choice is not always synonymous with improving their welfare. Allowed access to a variety of grazing, Nessie chose the most energy-rich (either because it was the most succulent or because it was simply ungrazed and therefore enticing) and made herself profoundly unwell in the process.

Some would liken her behaviour to that of a child in a sweet-shop, but this analogy somehow implies that she was disobeying rules. A better understanding can be arrived at if we simply remind ourselves that horses live from feast to famine. The rigours of a harsh winter will be withstood only by those that have cashed in on the benefits of the summer. The deposition of subcutaneous fat depends on consuming excess food in times of plenty. Native cobs and ponies are the closest relatives of the wild horses that roamed the northern Hemisphere thousands of years ago, and they evolved in such a way as to maximise the use of any resources. They were rarely faced with the kind of phenomenal gluts that are now associated with man; cereals were not harvested and stored in concentrated areas; and fires were not started to stimulate booms in the growth of grasses. Laminitis would have been very rare indeed as these ancient equids scraped a bare existence, and so the tendency to develop the dreadful condition has not been selected out of the population. The excesses of the domesticated environment are the main reason that we see so many laminitic animals these days.

The other possible contributing factor that singled out Nessie may have been that she was the best nourished of all the horses before she even left the field. As the boss, she would naturally get the best pickings and eat them more voraciously in the presence of the other horses.

Displacement behaviour

In essence, a displacement behaviour is one that is adopted by an animal that is prevented from performing another, more appropriate or preferred, behaviour. In the horse there are some notable examples of activities that can be used to identify thwarting and frustration.

Pawing at the ground is seen in horses that are prevented from moving forward – for instance, a stallion that is told to wait before mounting a receptive mare. Another example of displacement activity that may accompany pawing when a horse is thwarted by a barrier is snorting. Snorting seems to express the horse's frustration at being separated from a goal – for instance, a bucket of food that lies some distance away. To move towards the goal would be the most appropriate thing to do, but if that is not possible snorting and pawing are adopted as displacement strategies.

In the foaling mare, eating may be seen as a displacement activity, since it is not directly related to the job in hand and is thought by some to offer a distraction from the pain of contractions. However, a more direct link between the pain of foaling and the need to eat has been suggested: there is now some evidence that the sugars in food may raise the levels of circulating endorphins, the body's own pain-killing mechanisms.

Displays

Displays are seen in social circumstances in equine groups and, along with aggressive behaviour, are considered to be the origins of the 'airs above the ground', or high school, movements. The display that ensues when two horses meet involves a tremendous amount of elevation, along with stylised head and tail positions that alert other herd members to the prospect of a new affiliate and the possibility of hierarchical changes. The other reason for such elevated actions is to ensure that, as the elaborate posturing of a group display develops, manoeuvrability and surefootedness are maximised.

By watching the way in which horses posture and display, it is possible to imagine how they are seen by other horses. Each flick of the ears and elevation of the tail signifies forward or backward attention. The horse can also orientate his body to escape threats and kicks coming from one side or the other. Tail-swishing can signal irritation or a threat to kick out. In dressage competitions, it is interpreted as 'resistance', while racehorse owners regard it as a sign of being 'ungenuine'.

Warning signals help to minimise injury in the herd.

Question

I have a piebald vanner-type cob gelding called Taylor, whom everybody regards as rather common although I know that coloured horses are enjoying a sustained wave of popularity. He is very good in traffic because he used to belong to a family of gypsies, who always tethered their horses on the roadside. Very little seems to get him going but occasionally, when a strange horse trots past the field, he goes bananas with lots of flashy trotting and snorting. The most striking thing about these episodes is the way his tail carriage changes. He brings it right over his back just like an Arab, and I wish my friends could see him doing this because he looks really flash. Why does he do this with his tail?

Answer

The obvious answer to your inquiry is that he does this because he is excited. Of course, the next question is: Why should excitement make a horse do this?

Essentially, what you are describing is a very important display. Horses use tail postures and displays in many types of behaviour that have social, sexual or safety significance to other horses. For instance, the chances of a stallion spotting that a mare is in season are enhanced not only by the winking of her clitoris, but also by her distinctive lateral tail movements that accompany urination. Movement of the tail is integrated into defaecation and urination, both of which elicit interest in other horses.

Tail-switching, especially in a vertical direction, is an

important signal given before aggressive interactions like kicking. Such warning signals help to minimise injury to members of the group. Another example can be observed when horses are moving as a herd. Here it is important that signals be passed from one member of the group to the next, to avoid a pile-up. In such a situation elevation of the tail seems to indicate an intention to move faster, while lowering it is reckoned to signal the intention to slow down.

The context of Taylor's display is greeting. He is advertising his presence and hoping that the visitor will come closer to exchange pleasantries, snorts and squeals. Thankfully, any equine observer will pick up these cues rather than resorting to the sort of dismissive snobbery your friends have been guilty of. There's a lot to be said for being a horse, especially a piebald cob!

E

Eating

Question

I have been breeding Arabs for several years, and have witnessed a number of strange incidents when they are able to interact as a group. One behaviour pattern continues to baffle me, and so I was wondering whether you might be able to shed some light on it. Over the past two years, I have seen my youngsters occasionally gathering in a corner of one particular field with their heads to the ground. They do not spread themselves out in a normal grazing distribution, so I decided to investigate. When I got up close to them, I could see that they appeared to be licking a bare patch of soil. Their tongues were covered with mud, and when I got up really close to one filly I could hear her crunching grit. As you may imagine, that really set my teeth on edge. Could you explain what these strange episodes are all about?

Answer

Every year I receive a number of inquiries of this nature: the letters describe a short period, usually in the spring at turn-out time, when the horses and ponies in a particular field give undue attention to one part of the paddock – often a boggy area or the site of a felled tree. It may be that the soil in this spot is particularly heavily laced with fungal organisms which the horses find irresistible. However, it seems more likely that their absence from the field has meant that they have had to go without micronutrients (minerals or even vitamins) that happen to be present in that particular part of the field. The need to supplement dietary sodium has been suggested as the primary benefit of soil ingestion. A way of further investigating your horses' behaviour that might help to clarify this craving would be to take a couple of samples from the favoured patch and another three or four from nearby spots that are never selected. Then it would be a question of persuading a nutrition laboratory to run some analyses for the most common minerals (starting with sodium chloride). If samples from the licked areas were consistently higher compared with the normal sites, then you would have a complete answer.

You are quite right, it is rather cringe-inducing to witness horses grinding their way through anything other than plant material. But the horses themselves do not bat an eyelid as they savour the fine grit they have just licked from the ground, and they do not have the sensitive nerve endings in their molar teeth that we have in ours. Soil ingestion does not cause any harm, because it involves only tiny quantities relative to the volume of a horse's gut. Problems with equine bowels do arise, however, in paddocks with sparse grazing on sandy topsoil, and where rivers and streams with sandy bottoms are the only water sources. In some regions these sorts of topsoil can make sand colic horribly prevalent, though – thankfully – local vets become adept at diagnosing and treating it.

Another interesting consequence of keeping horses on minimal grazing within sandy areas is the erosion of the incisor teeth. The wear and tear of the side of the teeth nearest to the lips can even cause disputes when affected horses are bought and sold because the polished eroded parts are suggestive of crib-biting. The ensuing discussions about the true nature of the horse's behaviour can be lengthy and sometimes heated.

Question
My fourteen-year-old Irish Hunter, Dougan, has recently started eating his bed. I often find him picking at it in the morning when he has emptied his hay net. He is in regular work and his appetite can sometimes be difficult to satisfy. He generally avoids areas that are heavily soiled with dung, but I do worry that this habit cannot be good for him in the long run. Why does he do it?

Bed-eating is viewed with horror by some owners.

Answer

Bed-eating is viewed with horror by some owners because it has been described as a stable vice and because it often seems to involve the consumption of material that is soiled with faeces. The important point to remember here is that horses are likely to regard edible fibre that they find on the floor as food rather than bedding. In foraging for the next best thing when the hay in his net has disappeared, Dougan is behaving naturally. There is nothing in straw that is toxic – indeed, years ago most horses received straw as part of their daily food intake, in a chopped form – chaff. Largely because straw-chopping was labour-intensive, this practice suffered a steady decline in popularity until the appearance of so-called complete diets, mixes and mueslis. In these formulations the feed companies have been able to make less palatable low-calorie fibres like straw more attractive to their enqine consumers by dressing them with flavourings like molasses.

To my knowledge, there are no recorded cases of straw being solely responsible for intestinal blockages, but some owners will always regard bed-eating as unsafe. Even if a horse does eat a proportion of its own faecal matter, although distasteful to human observers this should cause no health problems. Since the bacteria present in a horse's manure originate in his own bowel, a secondary exposure to the same microbes, should they contaminate his food, is unlikely to cause a stomach upset.

The other point I must deal with is the reference you make to your horse finishing his hay ration. In this situation I could never recommend the elimination of an unwelcome activity without offering an alternative that meets your horse's behavioural needs. As you may know, the horse did not evolve to go for set periods every day without feeding. Indeed, in the field horses forage throughout the day and night – they never stop. Colic is so rare in grass-kept horses that I have to put two and two together and deduce that this system of ad lib foraging is better for them than artificially limited feeding regimes. Obviously, at grass horses move along as they feed and have to work to tug each mouthful from the ground. To mimic this and to lengthen the time that Dougan takes to eat a wedge of hay, you could try using more than one spot within the stable to feed him from. This way he could walk from one to another to get his fill. By placing one hay net inside another you can reduce the size of the holes through which the horse can pull out pieces of forage. Furthermore, you could suspend the hay net from a rubber ring – a loop made from an old bicycle inner tube, for instance – which would mean that the net would travel further before relinquishing its contents.

This brings me to the selection of a different type of bedding and to one of my oft-quoted points about stable management. Because all stabled horses are candidates for respiratory problems, I believe that the aim of all owners should be to minimise harmful dust levels at all times, rather than waiting for their animals to develop respiratory allergies. Therefore what has been called 'low-allergen management' is ideal for all horses – not just those that cough and splutter when exposed to fungal spores.

In the days before environmental awareness, I would have suggested that Dougan might feel very much at home on a bed made of peat. However, it appears that harvesting this resource causes a degree of damage to sensitive ecologies, and some owners would wish to consider this when selecting their horses' bedding. This being the case, your requirement for a bedding material that is hypoallergenic and of low palatability may be met by choosing shredded paper. To avoid a build-up in humidity, this should be refreshed regularly rather than being used as 'deep litter'.

Question

I have now replaced the rugs for my old cob mare, Osbourne, for the third time this winter. Every time I buy her a new night rug she sets about chewing it, starting with the chest area. I have tried a number of taste deterrents, but all to no avail. It seems that Osbourne has no taste and no respect for property, either. My friends have suggested that I try a muzzle. What do you suggest I do with her?

Answer

Although it has yet to be shown in horses, work in other species suggests that animals that are given control over their own heating and lighting, and even the extent to which they can gain access to members of their own species, will work to exercise their choices. This is done by giving them what are known as 'operant devices', which have to be manipulated in order to bring about a change in the animal's environment.

Horses that chew their rugs are very often simply too hot. Rug-chewing is most common among racehorses, which are regularly wrapped up like pass-the-parcel items in an attempt to prevent the long winter hairs from developing and thus spoiling the aesthetic appeal of a short shiny coat. You mention that your mare is old, without specifying her vintage or saying how much work is expected of her. If she is not in heavy work and not clipped, then the rugs she used to benefit from years ago may simply have become too ample for her own heat-conservation requirements. It may also be that, as she has aged, as happens with many horses

Osbourne has grown a longer coat. The added insulating capacity of a longer and hence thicker coat may be what prompted this form of disrobing. Furthermore, cobs are notoriously good at maintaining weight while on meagre rations, and it may be that Osbourne has laid down subcutaneous fat without your realising it. This also enhances a horse's capacity to conserve heat.

The chest area is not the only spot that horses pick on; some take great swipes at their flanks and come away with mouthfuls of jute or cotton. Devices that prevent them from actually reaching their rugs with their destructive teeth are likely to heighten the frustration level. You could try a material that cannot easily be grasped or, for that matter, torn.

Owners of horses that chew rugs often simply replace the rug in its entirety, without considering modifying the garment or simply tidying it up. Experimentation with different sorts of surcingles to secure the rug often pays dividends, since it can also be the straps rather than the excess body covering that prompt the behaviour in certain individuals. Turning the horse out as much as possible seems to bring about the biggest change. Obviously, in the teeth of a harsh winter we have to consider the use of heavy New Zealand rugs and close our eyes to the damage caused by hooves on wet ground. We tend to view stabling as the cheap alternative to extra ground, without questioning the effects that this can have on the mind of the creature that has to spend so much of its life inside the box.

Escape

When a new-born is caught and handled for the first time it responds with innate fear rather than curiosity. The foal's fear can be overcome by regular handling in the same way that any horse can be tamed, but we would do well to let the following example remind us of what the threat of no escape means to a horse. Escape from a trap is the animal's main means of survival, and the thwarting of this strategy leads to abject panic in many cases.

Question
How can I stop Elvis, my eight-year-old cob, breaking head-collars and lead-ropes. Every time he is tied up he just stands

square, sets his neck and leans back until something snaps and then he simply trots away. I have tried him with twine between the fence and the rope but this makes life too easy for him and he is gone within seconds. Why does he do this?

Answer

By trotting away from the scene of the crime your cob is making it quite plain that he finds being tied up unpleasant, and the things that happen to him when he is secured in this way do nothing to change his mind. It is possible that he was handled very roughly in a previous home, or even that he had facial surgery that required painful dressing changes (I have known several placid horses become thoroughly panic-stricken about being tied up just because they have had wounds drained and flushed as part of their post-surgical treatment). For this reason, anyone conducting aversive procedures such as injections should always first untie his patient.

The main thing is to realise that increasing the force that he needs to exert in order to escape will do nothing to convince Elvis that there is no need to panic. The more effort he puts into the task of escaping, the more the crown-piece of the head-collar is likely to hurt him and the greater will become his fear of being trapped. The old approach to a horse in this situation was to use chains and ropes to tie the neck to an immovable object like a log, the rationale being that in this way you could teach the horse that however hard he pulled he could not escape. The truth is that, as soon as the complexity of the trap is appreciated by the horse, blind panic intervenes. The risk of injury with this technique seems to rise as fast as the chances of any learning taking place plummet. I do not recommend such a 'cure'.

The idea should be to enable him to associate pleasant things with being tied up. For this programme you will need a roller and a lunge line. For safety reasons, revert to twine as a means of securing him to the fence. As soon as he is tied up, give him half of his normal concentrate ration. Then immediately attach the lunge line to the head-collar and pass it through a second loop of twine on the fence; then through the off-side ring of the roller, round the cob's quarters and finally through the near-side ring of the roller.

When he is finishing off his meal, stand at his near-side and get ready for an escape attempt.

As soon as he begins to put tension on the twine, pull the lunge line to drive him forward. He will be surprised – but as soon as he is standing still offer him the second half of his ration. The reward for pulling back – namely, his guaranteed escape – is thus removed while the advantages of staying beside the fence soon become obvious. Going through this routine every time he is tied up will soon effect a cure.

If, in the meantime, he is inadvertently allowed to break away without your supervision, be sure to coax him back to the fence line rather than fetching him yourself. Remember, being beside the fence line should be fun for him, not a continual threat. During the training programme don't leave him beside the fence without a hay net, and never use tying up as a means of restraint when you are doing anything unpleasant to him.

F

Farriers

It has been pointed out many times that horses rely on their feet for their safety. Escape from danger is only possible if their four limbs are free to provide the momentum for the getaway. Predatory pack-animals will often each seize a leg of their captured prey to prevent its disappearance. They also do this to diminish the effect of protective kicking, and to stop the prey being able to balance.

Expecting a foal to stand for a farrier to pick up and dress his feet for the first time is really pushing one's luck. The combination of being held by the head and having a foot grabbed amounts to a terrifying prospect for a young animal that has been programmed by evolution to escape from confinement. If the procedure of picking up the foot is not approached diplomatically, trouble can ensue for months and even years to come. The use of force or a twitch is to be avoided, since these will involve some discomfort – which will certainly be recalled for future reference. If the foal struggles throughout his first encounter with a farrier, he is likely to see the end of the procedure as the reward for his struggle rather than the point at which his feet were well trimmed. So future encounters are likely to be approached with the same desire to struggle for freedom.

The common-sense approach is to prepare in advance and take one step at a time, so that the odds are not stacked against the naive animal. Instead of asking him to cope with three threats at once – being restrained, meeting the farrier and having a leg held – approach the three stages individually. The establishment of a trusting bond between owner and horse is the most important prerequisite. Once this bond is in place, the owner can go about the business of getting the foal to tolerate being handled anywhere on its body, head or limbs. The appropriateness of scratches and rubs as rewards for remaining still will be obvious to anyone who has been around foals, especially when they are losing their baby coats. They can be sent into seventh heaven by a strategic scratching of the top of the croup.

When I am handling a foal that has yet to learn how to have his feet picked up, I always have a helper with me. When the foal is confident to have me around, I begin to ask him to stand while I lift a forelimb off the ground for a matter of two or three seconds. Letting the foal lean on me is tolerable at this stage. What I am aiming for is nothing more than the absence of any fuss. The helper has the vital role of rewarding the foal as soon as it has done well, and patience in this member of the team is crucial. It is important not to restrain movement of the foal's head, because he cannot see his flanks or hindquarters unless he is able to flex his neck. Letting him look round is an important part of teaching him that what is happening is safe. If he can see that the unfamiliar goings-on involve the person he trusts, then the chances of his panicking are considerably reduced. Before the foal is actually challenged by having its feet picked-up, the novelty of the farrier himself can be reduced by allowing the foal to experience the sights, sounds and smells associated with his visits to other horses.

All these habituation techniques involve patience, planning and time – commodities that are often in short supply on a busy yard – but the frustration and time that have to be expended on horses that have developed a phobia of farriers, and the dangers to which the animals are exposed, outweigh these factors many times over (as anyone who has owned an affected horse will tell you). Horses that cannot tolerate farriers are a danger to themselves (they are far more likely to get 'pricked' than a quiet horse) as well as to the people who deal with them. This is why horses are sold as being 'good to shoe' while owners tend to keep very quiet about those that are not. Horses that are difficult to shoe represent a considerable expense because naive farriers, from out of the area, have to be recruited (a wholly unfair approach) or sedatives have to be resorted to. The use of sedatives holds no guarantee of a gradual cure because, although the horse may be pacified while under the influ-

Horses that are difficult to shoe represent a considerable expense.

ence of the drug, it is unable to learn that the farrier is not simply there as an uninvited purveyor of torment.

What I have said about foals here also holds for older horses that have developed a phobia towards farriers.

Question

I bought a pony called Consul for my son and daughter last year, and have spent more than his purchase price in vet's bills. You see, the only way we can get him shod is to call the vet out at the same time as the farrier, so that the pony can be sedated. He is all right when we pick his feet out but as soon as he sees the farrier coming towards him he flips and cannot be held still at all easily. What can I do to curtail this expense?

Answer

Trying to hold a pony steady when he is gripped with fear is unlikely to be successful – it can even escalate his panic – and it is time to acknowledge that you are not as strong as he is. Do not be hard on yourself for labouring under this misapprehension: even some vets and farriers, who should know better, take a while to tumble to this eternal truth! For horses that are fearful the single most helpful thing that we can do is let them see what is going on. This is only possible when they can turn round to get a good view of who and what is around them.

There is every chance that your pony will change his ways with a counter-conditioning programme. It will involve mimicry on your part and, as ever, lashings of patience. The only implement you need is a hammer.

When Consul lifts his foot off the ground to have his feet picked out, start to hold and handle him in the same way as your farrier does for removing and nailing on shoes. After a short time he will acclimatise to these novel postures and you can enter phase two, which is to start tapping the shoe with the hoof-pick after you have picked out the hoof. Make sure you tap the wall of the hoof as well as the weight-bearing surface, to mimic knocking down the clenches. Do this routinely twice a day for a week before replacing the hoof-pick with the hammer.

Again, it is important to simply blend this into his normal routine, so remember to pick out his feet in your usual fashion before you start tapping with the hammer. If he can be fed at the end of each session, then so much the better. Once he is standing quietly for some serious clouts to the nail-heads, you can ring the farrier again. To make a smooth transition into real-life farriery, explain to your farrier what the programme that you are conducting involves and ask him to split his next visit into two on consecutive days. It helps if the appearance of the farrier is timed to coincide with your usual training or feeding times. On his first visit, just ask him to remove the old shoes and bid you good-day. Fitting and nailing on should be left for the following day. Although this may puzzle your farrier and may cost extra, it will ultimately make his life much easier and save you veterinary call-out fees and the price of sedatives.

Some owners report that finding a female farrier has been the other component of a cure, but this is never very easy. In fact, it seems that anything you can do to safely effect a change in your pony's response to the blacksmith-alert signals is worth a try. I have even had some clients go the whole hog and collect clippings from previous foot-dressings, which they then burned in an old saucepan every evening when the pony had his feed.

Flank-biting

Although by no means common, this is a very distressing sign and one that prompts several urgent inquiries to arrive in my office every year. The fact that all of the horses with the behaviour are male and most are stallions tells me a great deal about the nature of this problem. The prevalence of flank-biting inquiries in the spring and summer – in other words, in the mating season – is also an important clue as far as effective cures are concerned. Unlike flank-sucking in Dobermann pinschers, which is a stereotypic behaviour, flank-biting in horses is a form of mutilation that can come and go with the seasons and so defies classification as either 'stereotypic' or 'obsessive-compulsive'.

Question
I own a small Thoroughbred stud and am currently standing a nine-year-old stallion that I have owned for the past eighteen months. He had his own stable in the corner of the yard, which is very spacious because it is actually two foaling boxes knocked together. I show him in-hand three or four times a year and we keep him fit by lungeing him most days. What has prompted me to write is that about three months ago he started to snap at his flanks and has made quite a mess of the skin beyond his ribs on both his left and right sides. Sometimes he also kicks his belly, and I have called the vet out three times this year thinking that he had developed colic. The vet eventually operated on him to check for any tumours or blockages, but found nothing

abnormal inside. He suggested that I contact you for your thoughts on this matter.

Answer
Your stallion's behaviour is his only way of hinting to you that your current management regime does not suit him. The exercise needs of any horse are not confined to trotting round in circles on the end of a lunge line. Furthermore, the fact that he has a larger than normal box can do nothing to offset his need for ad lib grazing and social interaction.

Because they have evolved to use their teeth when they play-fight, dispute harem ownership and grip mares during sex, males are generally quicker to bite in frustrating circumstances than are female horses. In the absence of horseplay or other appropriate equine diversions, stallions sometimes direct this frustration against the nearest piece of horseflesh – their own.

The first time a horse manages to break his own skin in this way, the cause is straightforward frustration. As the broken skin heals it can become itchy, which can in itself lead to further nibbling. This cycle of skin-breaking and healing may be sufficient to perpetuate the behaviour. Therefore, once the true initiating causes have been removed, dressing the wounds and rugging up the horse are good ways of ensuring recovery. Neck cradles should be avoided, since they tend to escalate any generalised frustration by limiting the amount of normal movement the horse is capable of.

In the long term, sedative drugs are of little use in combating self-mutilative behaviour such as flank-biting, not least because they affect other, more natural behavioural characteristics such as the all-important libido of your stallion. But do not despair, because drugs that eliminate self-mutilation without causing sedation are currently being developed. The key to these research projects lies in identifying which pharmacological reactions occur in the horse's body when the behaviour is performed. It is thought that a brain-based chemical reward is generated when a horse flank-bites and that this may outweigh the skin-based pain associated with the behaviour. These rewarding chemicals may even provide an incentive for the behaviour while at the same time bringing some pain relief. At the moment the most likely identity of such a chemical is the body's own morphine equivalent – endorphin. This is confirmed by evidence from the United States, where considerable research has been conducted into flank-biting, suggesting that short-term cures may be effected with drugs that block the endorphin activity. However, there are problems with this approach to therapy because the drugs do not yet exist in oral forms and so have to be given by daily injection. Furthermore, we do not know enough about them to determine whether they eliminate the frustration that causes the behaviour or merely prevent the horse from expressing its frustration. If the latter, then we are not making life very much better for the affected animal.

The only effective therapy that I have found is to let the patient return to a more natural lifestyle. If he is allowed to run with mares, normal behaviour patterns return within a week and, of course, he can still be used for hand-mating where the needs of the mare dictate the use of this technique.

Flehmen

Question
I often find my New Forest pony mare, Wendy, curling her lip up in the field. She is kept with three other mares, one of which has a foal, and she seems to be the boss because she can send the others packing when food is put into the paddock. I thought it was stallions who are supposed to curl their lips when they smell a mare in season, so why is my mare doing it? Has she taken over the role of a stallion because she is the leader of the herd?

Answer
The curling of the upper lip in reaction to smells wafting from excrement or urine is called the Flehmen response. Wrongly interpreted by some owners as a sign of sexual interest and, even more off the mark, as a sign of amusement, this behaviour is seen in young and adult horses of both sexes. Indeed, it is especially common in foals during their first month of life when they can be spotted flehmening twelve or more times a day.

Flehmening is mainly a response to urine, but in horses

– unlike some other species – it does not require direct contact of the lips or tongue with the material giving off the chemicals. The wrinkling of the nose is thought to massage scents into the vomeronasal organ, which is designed to process odorous information from the environment. Also known as the lip-curl, this complex behaviour offers not only olfactory information to the performer but also a powerful visual cue to the observer. Signals can be left for other horses via scent messages, which are often added to by the recipient of the information once he has finished performing the flehmen response.

Friendship

Anxious to avoid anthropomorphism, ethologists tend not to use the term 'friendship' for non-sexual bonds that can be observed between horses. Instead, they favour expressions such as 'preferred associates', 'affiliates' and 'peers'. In deference to the purists I too will try to remember that I am a scientist, but I have retained the title of this section so that everybody knows what I am referring to.

In the first four weeks of life foals associate mainly with their dams, but from then on they tend to spend more and more time with their peers – that is, foals of a similar age-group. Play and mutual grooming are their main bonding activities, and since these tend to encourage interactions that work best with two participants discrete pairings start to emerge. Pairings can be between two colts, two fillies or a colt and a filly, but the nature of the mix has an influence on the type of bonding activities that the pair adopts. If a filly is one of the pair, mutual grooming tends to be the main affiliative behaviour and there will be little play-fighting or play-chasing. If both members of the pair are colts, there will be a great deal of classic 'locker-room' horseplay. This sort of interaction helps to fine-tune agility and prepare the musculature and the minds of the combatants for future pugilistic encounters as harem stallions.

At the onset of puberty, the social preference of young horses begins to shift. Sexual behaviour tends to come to the fore in exchanges with peers of the opposite sex. This is the stage at which the juveniles start to depart from the family group.

Affiliative behaviour between females is important,

because mares of an established band remain together even in the absence of a stallion. These affiliations may have their origins in foal associations, since fillies tend to spend more time with other fillies than with colts. Daughters also tend to remain closely associated with their dams. Pair bonds are often of particular importance among equids and are demonstrated by reciprocal following, mutual grooming and standing together. Most horses have preferred associates with whom they maintain proximity much more than with other herd members. Preferred associates also show more aggressive behaviour towards each other, but most of it takes a mild form such as the laying back of the ears rather than the more severe aggressions such as kicking, which are reserved for the other herd members.

Coalitions are an important part of the social network within 'bachelor herds', which develop as halfway houses for males that have been ejected from their natal bands. The development of pair bonds and of larger unified groups among unrelated individuals seems to be an important co-operative defence mechanism. This is recognised in zoological collections, where such associations allow the safe mixing of young Przewalski horses with older, potentially dangerous, stallions.

G

Grazing

The earliest reports of grazing in a new-born foal come from a famous study of New Forest ponies that was completed in the early 1970s by Stephanie Tyler. She recorded a foal nibbling at grass for a total of fifteen minutes while its dam struggled for forty minutes to expel the afterbirth. The increase in grazing activity is a gradual one. During daylight hours, foals of four months of age may graze for 25 per cent of each hour, while by twelve months this has increased to 75 per cent. Interestingly, foals that have been orphaned do not graze as readily as foals that enjoy their mother's company.

Grazing, as we have already seen, takes up such a significant part of a horse's day that it is as important to it as sleeping and television are to modern Western man. Unlike other herbivores such as cows or rabbits, which indulge in regurgitation or specialised coprophagy, equids have only one chance to process their food – so the chewing process is all-important. It is the milling and grinding that goes on in the horse's mouth that breaks open as many plant cell walls as possible to release the cellular contents for absorption by the fore-gut. The cell walls are digested by helpful bacteria in the large bowel, but this stage is rather late in the alimentary day for the efficient absorption of the cell contents.

Horses are often described by farmers as wasteful grazers, when compared with cattle and sheep. The fastidious way in which horses develop latrine areas certainly contributes to this bad publicity – grazing usually occurs in areas that are free from faecal contamination. This means that longer grass develops in these rather repugnant areas, referred to as 'roughs', while most of the other grass is kept much shorter. Before defaecating horses usually walk to the longer grass where they drop their dung, which is why these patches are also referred to as latrine areas. The only exception to this general rule is found with foals, who seem unaware of the protocol and even graze in the toilets!

In avoiding areas contaminated with faeces, horses reduce the risk of picking up worm larvae but they end up with a shortage of 'lawn' areas that can be efficiently grazed. The process of harrowing really confounds them – if they are still present – since it serves to spread the faecal contamination around the whole paddock. But the worm larvae are exposed to the elements more rapidly than they would be in natural circumstances, and so they probably die off before they can be picked up by grazing mouths.

Selection of grasses and herbs continues throughout the grazing period. Horses may fine-tune this selection process by intermittently searching for more fibrous or mineral-rich items such as tree bark. Oak and ash seem to be particular favourites, but it is not clear why this should be. It has been suggested that animals may be capable of self-medication with plants known to have healing properties; this has yet to be studied in horses, but we do know that patches of soil hold particular appeal for short periods when a group of horses arrives in a new paddock. As mentioned earlier, this suggests that these areas hold reserves of trace elements which are relished by horses if they have gone without them for some time. The same process is exhibited in a more elaborate fashion by cattle in South Africa, which are known to crave minerals to the extent that they will chew the skeletal remains of deceased relatives in order to replenish their bodies' own stocks of certain trace elements.

Grazing is a behaviour that can be influenced by social facilitation – the process whereby a behaviour is initiated by, or increases in rate or frequency with, the presence of another animal doing the same thing.

Grinding

Question
Samba, my aged Welsh Section A pony mare, has recently started to grind her teeth after a meal. She does not seem to drop food while she does it and appears to be perfectly

normal in all other respects. I do find the habit quite irritating, and I wonder if you know of any way to prevent it?

Answer
Occasionally, teeth-grinding can be related to unsatisfied feeding requirements and, as with other oral-based stereotypic behaviours such as crib-biting, can be alleviated only by the provision of ad lib forage. But if there have been no recent changes in management and given that Samba is aged, stereotypy is an unlikely explanation for the sudden appearance of the signs that you describe. You should therefore consider ill-health as a possible reason for your mare's behaviour. Your vet will be able to investigate the various possibilities, which include discomfort from oral abnormalities such as hooks on teeth and the resultant ulcers. The slopes on the surfaces of horses' cheek teeth are never perfectly symmetrical, and as a consequence sharp protrusions can develop on either side of the molar arcade. Whether on the left or right, these spurs usually lie beside the cheek rather than alongside the tongue, and in this position can cause discomfort every time the horse chews his food.

Beyond this, it is believed that any source of chronic discomfort can lead to teeth-grinding. For example, some vets have reported the behaviour in association with ongoing colics and grass disease. It is not clear why this should be, but it is tempting to speculate that the behaviour can distract the patient: just as, after hitting a thumbnail with a hammer, humans feel the curious need to jump up and down (with or without the inclusion of colourful language), teeth-grinding in horses may be a way of activating other pathways in the nervous system – a process known as 'gaiting'. After a thorough dental examination, your vet will discuss what tests he can do to identify any underlying cause of Samba's habit.

Grooming
Grooming may be categorised by ethologists as maintenance, comfort or social behaviour, depending on its context. Because horses do not seem to be able to recognise themselves in a mirror, it seems likely that they do not have any concept of self-image. So when they groom themselves they do not do so to improve their appearance, but mainly for comfort. There are also survival advantages to regular

grooming: for instance, it helps to maintain the quality of the coat by removing dead hairs and stimulating the secretion of natural waterproofing oils.

As far as the horse himself is concerned, there are a number of strategies that he can adopt to become more comfortable. Rolling sets the hairs in the desired direction and breaks up patches of sweat and caked mud. However, its effect on ectoparasites is minimal, since lice and mites have adapted to occupy a position under the canopy of outer hairs in the coat and are therefore more or less invulnerable. Furthermore, they are certainly not affected by moisture and so the water content of mud in which their hosts roll has negligible effects.

Allogrooming is the term given to the grooming of other individuals, and where this takes place with both parties benefiting to a similar extent it is known as mutual grooming. French researchers working with semi-feral horses in the Camargue have recently shown that mutual grooming is associated with a reduction in the heart rates of the participants. So it may be useful not only as a means of reaching inaccessible parts but also as a sort of pacifier, or relaxant. The shoulders and withers are the parts of the body most often groomed in this way. While the activity is most common among juveniles, most horses tend to establish regular grooming partners; the more submissive member is most likely to initiate the exchange, but the dominant member of the pair ends the session. The peak of this behaviour among foals is reached when they are three to four months old. A similar sort of mutually beneficial behaviour pattern is seen when horses stand head-to-tail swishing flies away from each other's heads.

When the teeth are used in grooming, it seems to be more often the lower jaw that is more effective – for instance, for scratching the elbows. The mouth is also involved in grooming the barrel, with both licking and snapping action. The latter is particularly used as an anti-insect manoeuvre; newborn foals can combat attacks from insects in this way within two hours of being born. Nibbling lower parts of the legs such as the pasterns is not very easy for an adult horse, and is seldom witnessed – only if he is feeling extremely itchy, perhaps as a result of a lice infestation, does an adult horse regularly devote himself to this task.

Shaking, which involves the rapid vibration and rotation of the body surface, helps to remove loose hairs and dust from the coat. In localised areas the horse can also quiver its skin – for example, over the withers as a means of disturbing irritating insects.

Question
Ever since I bought my Arab mare Brigitte as a yearling, she has been difficult to groom. She starts fidgeting almost as soon as I tie her up and gets particularly upset when I groom her face and her groin. I have tried using fine brushes on these sensitive parts but it seems to make little difference. Why is she so ticklish in these areas?

Answer
The muzzle is sensitive because it is responsible for a great deal of tactile sensation: for instance, in feeling the proximity of the ground when a horse is grazing, and the direction of the mare's hair growth when her foal is seeking the udder for a drink. The groin, too, has a low threshold for tactile stimulation because it is the location of sensitive organs – the udder, or the sheath and testicles. These areas are hairless because they are designed for interaction with other animals, and so need to dry easily and to provide minimal sanctuary for parasites so as to inhibit their spread from one individual to another. And because it is hairless, the skin that covers these parts is also designed to detect the presence of other horses and to be sensitive to the movement of insects.

Because we are talking here about reflex thresholds there is little you can do to modify Brigitte's behaviour. All I would recommend is that you appreciate why these areas are sensitive and adapt your grooming technique accordingly. Many people find that the only way to clean these parts without annoying their horses is to groom without any brushes. Although this is a messy business, it has the advantage that it seems to help strengthen the bond between horse and handler.

Head-shaking

Question
I have a seven-year-old Anglo-Arab gelding that has competed successfully in dressage competitions ever since I bought him last year. However, over the last month or so he has started throwing his head around whenever I ask him to go in an outline. I have tried him with a variety of bits and have even had his teeth rasped, but I have been unable to produce any improvement. In fact, the whole thing is becoming quite serious because he throws his head back to the extent that it hit me in the face last week and gave me a nose-bleed. Why do you think he has suddenly started doing this?

Answer
This is your horse's way of relieving an ongoing irritation – any head-shaking horse is trying to make himself more comfortable. Head-shaking is often, though not always, restricted to ridden exercise including certain types of schooling work, such as when a rider asks for poll flexion. Furthermore, head-shakers sometimes get worse at certain times of day and certain times of the year. Because there are so many causes of this syndrome, it would be foolish to pick one out of the hat in my reply in the hope that it was the right one. My advice is to start keeping a logbook of what conditions make the shaking behaviour worse. Your records should include a score out of ten for the severity of the shaking. Where the habit is confined to ridden work, as in your case, it's important to include details such as the types of plants growing in the different schooling areas and the type of bit the horse is wearing. In addition, it is also

... any head-shaking horse is trying to make himself
more comfortable.

helpful to monitor his response to being lunged in areas
with different vegetation, and the effect of changing riders.

You are quite right to take this problem seriously: not only
does it affect the performance and value of your gelding, but
it also brings with it the risk of physical injury. There are
numerous reasons for head-shaking, many of which centre
on equitation and saddlery, while others involve the immun-
ological and psychological status of the horse. The decision
about which to blame in each individual case rests entirely
with your vet.

There are a number of diagnostic procedures that can be
performed to get to the root of each horse's problem. These
include the use of X-rays and fibre-optic endoscopes that
give the veterinary surgeon detailed information about any
anatomical changes that may have occurred inside the nasal
cavity. Another procedure that may be employed is a short-
lasting nerve block that freezes the nerves carrying information from the nose to the brain. If the behaviour abates
in response to the nerve block the vet can begin to specify
where the irritation is coming from. In many cases, when
there is a clear positive result with this test, the investigations

stop here and a tentative diagnosis of allergic rhinitis is made, the treatment for which is a surgical procedure called neurectomy (nerve-removal) which aims to permanently eliminate sensation in these nerve bundles. The success claimed for this operation is impressive, but certainly relies on the correct selection of candidates.

Hearing

The mobility of equine ears means that hearing can easily be studied in scientific tests. The hearing ability of horses varies, but it appears to be reduced in those over fifteen years of age compared with those under ten. At its most basic, a mere lack of ear movement is one of the first signs of deafness. Since deaf horses are also slightly more dependent than normal ones on vision, they tend to be seen rolling their eyes and looking around in an almost paranoid fashion.

Most of the sounds heard by horses are within the ranges of frequency and amplitude used by humans. However, horses appear to be able to detect a broader range of sound. For example, they have been heard to vocalise before earthquakes. These vocalisations are apparently in response to very high and very low frequency sound vibrations, which they pick up before humans detect any ground tremors.

Heat

Because horses have evolved to survive in a wide variety of climates, they have developed a number of strategies for coping with extreme heat. These include sheltering from the direct rays of the sun and being able to sweat quite readily without the stimulation of exercise. (Recent reports of feral horses being found in desert terrain in Namibia as a legacy of German occupation many decades ago seemed to defy understanding until an ancient well was discovered in their home range.) Simply standing beside water is thought to have some cooling effect.

In drought conditions in Australia horses are not regarded as the greatest survivors, since their ability to conserve water resources is poor. They are often found dying in water sources, which consequently become repugnant to the other members of the herd and cease to be available for life-saving rehydration.

Homing

When they are away from their patch horses seem to have an innate desire to relocate to their home ranges, and they do this with their senses of smell and vision. The way in which bands of horses travel back and forth from grazing areas to distant water sources is regarded as an illustration of their ability to memorise landmarks – memory is the only alternative to trial-and-error learning for horses attempting to return home. However, this topographical approach to homing is probably less important than the sense of smell, which is thought to bring more horses home than any visual imagery. Retracing previous routes is a task that horses perform with their noses lowered to check for olfactory clues, and one that is very much at the mercy of the prevailing wind. The importance of wind direction was demonstrated in the 1950s by Moira Williams, who conducted behavioural research with her own family of performance horses. She found that when she allowed them to wander off to a distance of several kilometres from home, they always tended to orientate themselves into the wind, regardless of the direction of their stable yard. This suggests that the horses in question were not very good at homing, or perhaps they were not highly motivated to come home.

Motivation to return to familiar company or, for that matter, surroundings will depend on prior experience of separation and current influences such as fear. Horses that were weaned by being taken away from both their dam and their home range are known to be the most likely to be distressed by subsequent changes in surroundings. Their previous experience and extraordinary memory for negative stimuli have the capacity to elicit vocalisation as well as what appears to be mild panic. Naturally, not all horses that are traumatically weaned are going to respond to being away from home in this way, but the predisposition they have for distress is understandable.

In addition to previous aversive experiences associated with novel environments, current fear is the other catalyst for relocation behaviour. This is why the bolting horse very often heads for home – he depends not only on speed for his survival but also on his memory of how to find his home range.

I

Imprinting
Imprinting is a special sort of learning that occurs for a limited period during the early life of many animals. It establishes a long-term association between the young animal and its dam. Imprinting is seen in many animals that rely on maternal effort and parental presence for their survival. Its most graphic representations are seen in birds like ducks and geese, which are rapidly able to follow their mother out of the nest. These babies are especially vulnerable to predation, and it is vital that they learn to follow their mother rather than some hungry wild dog who would just love to have a flock of bite-sized birdie snacks follow him back to his den.

The mechanism that has evolved to avoid becoming such an easily picked up take-away has to do with timing. Baby animals are susceptible to imprinting for only a short period in their early life; the idea is that if, during this time, they are presented with repeated images of their mother, this is the figure that they will follow and run to for comfort. The sensitive period in foals has been delineated at around the second hour after birth. The selection of sexual partners later is also influenced by the associations the foal makes at this stage in its life.

It is also worth remembering that a similar bonding process operates to allow the mother to identify her foal. This bonding takes longer for mares, beginning at birth and lasting for days rather than hours. Once this attachment between mother and infant has been formed, it is difficult to persuade her to accept any other foal. The evolutionary advantage of this behavioural strategy is that it helps to protect the infant and to reduce the possibility of mismothering.

There are occasional reports in the literature of foals directing their attachment towards bizarre objects, apparently just because they are of a similar size to a mare. For example, Stephanie Tyler describes a New Forest foal that appeared to have bonded to a tree rather than to its dam. It is thought that in cases such as this the dam is likely to abandon the foal with the equine version of righteous indignation. However, if the foal's imprinting is redirected towards the dam early enough, a successful maternal-infant bond can be achieved.

Insects
Insects cause changes in the behaviour of individual horses and in that of groups. The irritation caused by flies should not be underestimated, since apart from eliciting foot-stamping and tail-swishing it can mean that some horses come in from the field keyed up or with mild exhaustion. It has been suggested that these forms of behaviour may serve as signals to other horses and help to delineate bothersome areas within a patch of grazing. While this is possible, the presence of flies does not seem to deter the arrival and co-operation of other herd members. In fact, in group situations horses have been shown to develop co-operative strategies that reduce insect irritation. The most familiar of these is standing head-to-tail, while other groups co-operate *en masse* by reducing the collective surface area exposed to flies; they do this by facing in towards each other while taking turns to walk around the perimeter of the circle, using their tails to brush away insects on their herd-mates. The formation of large groups of feral horses during fly seasons is in itself an effective means of reducing the number of fly-bites per horse.

Another technique that horses use to reduce the effects of insects is to seek bodies of water unsuitable as a launching pad for flying insects. For example, Assateague Island ponies in the United States will stand in breaking waves. In the UK a similar strategy is adopted by New Forest ponies who will stand on tarmac to avoid flies – insects, preferring the cover of vegetation, tend to be less prevalent on the road. Finally, movement can help in the fight against insect damage and so, like gadding calves, horses are often seen to take off at speed with their tails thrashing away at the persistent pests.

The size of the insect bears little relationship to the level of damage that it can inflict. While horseflies that bite can leave their victim looking like a shrapnel survivor, the allergic reactions that some horses have to midge bites are often far worse. This is especially so if the horse has allergic dermatitis, or sweet itch. The damage that a horse can do to itself when afflicted with sweet itch is always a distressing reminder of how very irritating midge bites are and how frenzied an animal can become when faced with this sort of eczematous disease. There is a hereditary component to this disorder, and it also appears that horses of certain colours, especially chestnuts, are more likely to show signs of it.

J

Jibbing

When a horse jibs, he is resisting forward motion, and he does so by simply standing still and refusing to advance. Most horses do this from time to time, often merely to get a better look at something novel. On occasions this is perfectly acceptable and not something I would wish to eliminate completely from a horse's behavioural response, since the horse that looks after himself in this way is one day going to save you from a hazard that you had failed to spot. By way of an example, allow me to indulge myself by recounting a simple story from the Australian Bush which involves the three horses that a friend of mine and I took on an eight-week trek along old drovers' trails in Victoria and New South Wales.

One afternoon we reached the remains of a bridge that was marked on our map but had since been washed away. So we were forced to ford the river at a spot a little farther upstream. Two of the horses, Bruce and Drake, refused to approach the bank, so I hopped onto our very obliging pack-horse, Mac, who agreed to proceed where his peers had jibbed. Within seconds we were both disappearing into quicksand and had to be towed out by the dry crew members behind us. Although he had been the most obedient, Mac had exposed himself as the least sensible equine member of the expedition. By baulking, the two riding-horses had averted a double disaster because towing them out would have been beyond little Mac.

Refusing to 'walk on' is therefore the most innocuous form of jibbing. The others include rearing and even running backwards.

Question
Over the last five weeks, my five-year-old Anglo-Arab, Roy, has started to jib whenever I ask him to turn right at the end of our driveway. On his way home he comes along the same stretch of road without any problems, and will happily turn left at the end of the drive. The disobedience started with him spooking at a plastic carrier-bag in a gateway just down the lane, to the right of our main entrance. The next morning brought the next sign of trouble with him just standing still, but now he withdraws into himself, loses all contact and rears, while sometimes throwing in the occasional buck. I have given him several good thrashings but he does not seem to have learned his lesson. In fact, rather than getting better, he seems to be getting more troublesome and downright dangerous. Given the fact that this is happening on my doorstep and that I am a freelance riding instructor, I find this extremely embarrassing. What do you suggest?

Answer
While you have been punishing the behaviour you regard as unacceptable, you may also have confirmed to Roy that the gateway is threatening. Very few mothers would drag a screaming child to see a violent film and expect him or her to emerge having lost a long-engrained fear of the sight of blood. Why is it, then, that we regard punishment as a way of approaching fear in horses? A whip can be used to support a leg aid that may have gone unheeded, but should not be used for thrashings. What worries me is the number of riders who apply the whip without asking themselves: With what, exactly, could the horse be associating the pain it feels? (I am, however, convinced of the benefits of carrying a whip while hacking, especially in traffic, since many horses can be guided out of the path of oncoming traffic only with the encouragement of a whip.)

To put it simply, turning left when he is returning has become more inviting for Roy. The fact that he walks back along the road so contentedly is related to the fact that the sights and smells on a given road change so much depending on the direction you are travelling. You can use this to your advantage when habituating Roy to the gateway, which is what seems to be at the root of his problem.

The exercise I want you to adopt is designed to eliminate the cultural or routine aspect of the behaviour difficulty – the fact that the gateway presents a problem only when faced in one direction. To overcome this, it is important that you do not start each day's ride with an argument: disobedience is far less common after a period of harmony. So, for the next few weeks, you should begin your hacks by turning left when you get to the end of your drive so that Roy makes only homeward-bound journeys past the gateway. He will then have done as he was asked for an extended period before you both reach the problem area, and you will have him settled into a more cooperative frame of mind than appears to have been the case of late. When you get to the gateway, ask him to stop before he does so of his own accord, let him look around and then execute three or four circles in both directions, at the walk. This will teach Roy that the sight of the gateway is not an automatic cue to put up his objections.

Once you are certain that he is willing to move in circles alongside the gateway, all you have to do is make these tracks day by day more egg-shaped (with the gateway being the base of the egg). Remember to ride in both directions, and introduce trotting on the long sides of your track. Within three weeks Roy will be trotting towards the bogeyman gateway and you may safely reintroduce right turns at the start of your rides.

Jogging

The homing instinct is well recognised in horses; it seems to have its origins in their need to get back to base after sorties to distant resources such as water. The increase in pace shown by some horses when they sense familiar smells and landmarks is a sign that they are keen to return to their home range, where they are more secure because they are familiar with all the escape routes, vantage points and dead ends.

Question
My point-to-pointer always jogs home, which means that I'm completely exhausted by the time I get off him after a ride. He starts the jogging business after his first canter of the day, but it certainly gets worse when we begin to head for

home. If I ask him to walk he may do two walk steps before resuming the jog. If I ask him to trot he just takes advantage by going faster and faster. Why does he do this?

Answer
The clearest answer to this question is 'Because he wants to', but to offer a greater understanding of his behaviour I would point out that horses have not evolved to settle in areas that are distant from home. The urgency shown by feral horses that have been rounded up, moved and then released, to return to their home range is quite remarkable. Many have been recorded galloping, swimming and going without food until they are close to home. So the increase in your Thoroughbred's pace when he detects that he is going home can be put down to his increased motivation to get back to his home range with its familiar company, safety and food. The fact that this motivation is expressed as a jog brings me to the other point that needs to be made – that jogging is a learned pace. Furthermore, the jog is an undesirable gait not only because it is exhausting for riders but also because it plays havoc with fitness programmes, and it is believed to abbreviate the working life of the horse.

The only effective therapy I have found for dealing with this behaviour is to concentrate on its habituation component, since its motivational aspects are more or less beyond modification. The idea is to teach the horse to travel at a similar pace without adopting the unwelcome gait. As the first step in accomplishing this, only allow him to travel in his favourite direction (homeward-bound) when he is walking. If he starts to jog, let him – but only when he is pointing away from home.

You will need to plan very short rides for the period of this programme, because under this regime even the smallest journey can take some horses a couple of hours. Any trotting you do should be a rising trot, since he has learned to ignore the difference between sitting and attempts to reduce the pace with your seat. Using this technique, most owners can persuade even the fizziest horses to use 'approved' gaits.

K

Kicking

In feral contexts, horses kick with their hindlegs in challenges and in self-defence. They will kick out, most often with a single limb, when they are annoyed – for instance, by flies. These limb swings are often directed towards parts of the abdomen that are beyond the reach of a swishing tail. Abdomen-directed kicks are also seen when a horse is experiencing colic. Colicky horses display this behaviour because the discomfort they are feeling is centred on the belly, and they kick at it in the same way as they would deal with a huge fly.

Kicking in the stable is generally seen in horses with a low irritation threshold. Traditionally, rodents were blamed for this behaviour. This may still occasionally be the case, although in my experience horses are extremely tolerant of familiar small animals that represent no threat. An irritating neighbour is a more likely cause of kicking in the stable. The yard manager who, in confined situations, puts two unaffiliated horses side by side for the convenience of feeding and cleaning regimes can be responsible for considerable misery. Hierarchical disputes conducted over the stable door, or through the bars and grilles for that matter, are rarely completely resolved and seem to form a large part of the combatants' daily schedule unless they are otherwise occupied. In the case of horses that have never been turned out together but can see one another through bars and grilles, the key to a reduction in neighbour-related antagonism is to have them feeding as far apart as possible, and preferably out of sight of one another.

With a stable-kicking horse, it is important to eliminate the possibility that the behaviour has become stereotypic. As we have seen with crib-biting (and as we shall also see later with weaving), these behaviours, once established, can come to exist quite independently of their initiating causes. It is worth remembering that stereotypies do not have to be bizarre – the constant repetition of a normal behaviour can also constitute an abnormality. To borrow an example from my work with dogs: we would all recognise flank-sucking as a stereotypy, but we would not necessarily see the dog who stands at a gate barking repetitively as having a similar problem.

Before becoming stereotypic, a kicking horse may have been exposed to a high degree of fly irritation, or it may have experienced frustration at a lack of exercise or turn-out. The remedy, as with all of these behaviours, is to provide appropriate stimulation for the animal in an attempt to normalise the way in which it spends its day. For most horses this means increasing the time it has available to socialise – for instance, in a loose-school set-up – and maximising the time it spends foraging. Some owners have reported success with attempts to distribute their horses' food around the stable. Similarly, zoos with monkeys that show stereotypies report that keepers have found that hiding morsels of food in puzzle-feeders reduces the performance of the abnormal behaviours more than, say, providing an old car tyre for the animals to play with. The provision of relevant 'work' seems to bring greater benefits, when we attempt to normalise an animal's schedule, than does irrelevant 'play'.

Question

I have owned my eight-year-old Hanoverian mare since she was weaned. She is extremely talented and has taken me to the very top in my area's intermediate dressage competitions. I keep her at livery at a good local riding school, where she is regarded as something of a celebrity because she has so much flare. I don't like to turn her out into the paddock for too long because she is so valuable. In fact, she is always keen to come in from the paddock but seems to get bored very easily in the stable. She tends to get very wound up when other horses go past her stable, and she often 'piaffes' and kicks the stable walls. She is particularly bad when she is in season. What can be done to calm her down?

There is always the worry about the risk of injury in
the field.

Answer

You are obviously very proud of your mare and are aiming
to keep her as safely as possible. I suspect that when you
turn her out at grass there is always the worry about the risk
of injury in the field, which would be a setback to your
competition plans. All the same, I have to say that turning
her out in a paddock as well as increasing her workload will
be the best way of improving her behaviour. If you could
find an aged pony mare without hind-shoes, the chances of
her kicking your strapping Hanoverian through the fence
would be minimal. To be extra safe, you could fit your mare
with brushing and over-reach boots for her time at grass.

The mare's reasons for wanting to come in have more to
do with wanting a tasty feed than wanting to be housed.
But, if the weather or ground really do not suit her, you
should improve her living conditions before she comes in
for any length of time. The most important improvement

that you could make would be to provide her with company in an adjoining box, and allow the two horses to communicate through bars and grilles.

The other point appears to be the lack of sufficient space to accommodate her kicking habit. Wall-kicking is a significant cause of hock and back injuries and is something that should be tackled promptly. So if you can find a foaling box or a corner box in a yard that provides appreciably more space, you could modify it so that your mare was unable to reach the walls themselves. You might consider getting some 'swinging bales', which are beams that can be suspended from the ceiling of the box to hang about a metre (three feet) from the ground. At this height they are too high for a Hanoverian to get her hindlegs hooked up on, but I would take the extra precaution of suspending them with baler twine which will readily snap in an emergency, rather than anything too robust such as a chain.

L

Leadership

Leadership is a concept that evades definition as far as equine behaviour is concerned. This is because different horses within an established group can be seen leading that group in different circumstances.

Foals have an inquisitive nature that allows them to learn so many important lessons about things as diverse as food, herd-mates and danger – lessons that are essential if they are to integrate successfully into the herd's environment. Foals can lead simply by wandering. This does not mean that the movement of bands of horses is at the mercy of whimsical youngsters: a foal that is heading towards danger is very often retrieved by the harem stallion. Equally, when subordinates initiate a change in direction they are often seen stopping to allow a dominant herd member to overtake and assume the lead. This is how mares lead – by initiating movements of the harem towards resources like food and water. In many instances, it simply involves a hungry or thirsty mare travelling in the direction of the resource and eliciting social facilitation (a sort of mimicry) in her peers. Without necessarily being the dominant member of their groups, stallions move harem members away from threats such as an alien group, a strange male or an advancing predator. So, when a harem is on the move, its stallion is often seen at the rear of the group while a senior mare is usually the one to have initiated the change in location.

In conclusion, it seems that it is not very helpful to label a horse as the leader of a group. It is a context-specific role, and bears little correlation to rank.

Licking

Licking forms an important part of dental and facial hygiene for horses, and movement of the tongue and nibbling with the incisors are components of their grooming behaviour. However, when two horses groom one another licking is very rare, because the partners in a mutually beneficial bond of this sort prefer nibbling, which is a rather more definite activity than licking. Licking is also a prelude to mounting, when a stallion is making his final checks on the receptivity of his mare before copulation.

The nosing, smelling and licking of nearby objects are often seen as a part of the new-born foal's pre-nursing explorations. These are also directed at his dam, who gets her share of nibbles and licks before the foal settles into his first concerted suckle. The new mother also does a great deal of licking, which helps to both dry the foal and establish a strong bond between mother and infant. Indeed, for many months to come the nursing mare will turn round to smell and lick her foal's hindquarters when he returns to her for a drink. This is her way of ensuring that his odours and flavours are the same as those that she first encountered when she licked at the amniotic fluid on the ground around her, the result of her waters breaking.

The other example of licking behaviour that we see in horses at grass is salt-licking and soil-licking. These are important ways in which they can supplement reserves of sodium chloride that are depleted by body functions such as sweating. Interestingly, excessive salt-licking is also observed as one of the abnormal behaviour patterns of horses maintained on 'complete diets' – yet another illustration of how such diets, while providing sufficient nutrients, may yet fail to meet a horse's need for oral activity.

Question

I have a Dartmoor pony called Prince, who is kept at grass with three Shetlands and a donkey. Every time I go to see him, he licks the palms of my hands for ages and ages. It doesn't seem to matter whether I've given him a titbit or not, he just goes on licking. It tickles and makes my hands very slippery, but I don't mind because he really is very gentle. What I would like to know is why does he do this?

Answer

This is a common question but, as you point out, never a cause of concern. Licking seems to be a feature of horse behaviour that some horses show while others do not. We also know that some are very fond of playing with their tongues and there are even some that can blow raspberries by vibrating their tongues between their teeth.

The behaviour that you describe seems to be directed towards you rather than the environment, so it is worth bringing to mind the situations under which one horse licks another in feral settings. The prevalence of licking certainly seems to rise where mothers and foals are concerned, but this seems inappropriate in your case. Since the bond that exists between you and your pony is similar to the affiliation between companions in a group, another possibility is that Prince is trying to start a bout of mutual grooming with you. But this too seems unlikely, because these behaviours rarely persist unless they are reciprocated – that is, if the companion does not return the compliment, the first horse soon stops wasting valuable time and effort that is of no benefit to himself. Furthermore, bonded horses usually nibble rather than lick one another.

This process of elimination leaves us with the other instance of licking that is seen in horses at grass: salt-licking. And this is the most likely explanation since, even without exerting yourself, you are likely to pass sweat on to your skin. This occurs all over the body, but is concentrated in certain areas including the palms of the hands. All sweat contains salt, and it dries on the surface of your skin in an invisible layer. Horses have a special talent for finding tiny quantities of salt, a sense known as 'salt wisdom', and this is what allows them to find traces of sodium chloride on human skin. In this way, Prince is replacing salt that he lost through sweat with salt that his owner has lost in the same way. I would recommend that for Prince's own good you buy him a salt/vitamin/mineral-lick and say goodbye to most of the licking business.

Loafing

Loafing merits a mention in any consideration of horse behaviour because it takes up such a great deal of the typical horse's day. This is the pastime that horses resort to when

they have met their needs for food, water and companionship. Stallions, which spend less time lying on the ground
than mares, seem especially fond of it. Essentially the most
common form of rest, loafing is the state of relaxation somewhere between alertness and snoozing. It is seen not only
in feral horses but also, of course, in domestic ones when
they are in the paddock and, especially, in the stable.

Sunning is also a feature of this state of semi-wakefulness,
and is something that contented horses studiously indulge
in whenever climates suit. Unfortunately, the stabled horse
has limited access to this luxury and can really only doze
with his head over the stable door to catch what rays are
available. At liberty, he can find suntraps and orientate himself at right angles to the sun's rays to maximise their warm-
ing effect, while taking an occasional peek at the world
around.

When at grass, much of the social life shared by a group
of horses is conducted as they loaf around the paddock
together. As long as there is no pressing need to graze, the
members of a domestic band will move close to one another
and luxuriate in each other's company, enjoying the freedom to mutually groom and fly-swat.

M

Masturbating

Some scientists believe that sexual stimulation may occur in mares when they use fixed objects such as fence posts and shrubs to rub against their buttocks, tail and vulva. The possibility that self-gratification is involved here is suggested by the fact that mares engaged in this form of rubbing sway their heads from side to side and quiver their lips, in the same way as they would during free copulation. In stallions and geldings masturbation is rather more obvious because they rub their erect penis against their belly, sometimes to the extent of ejaculation. Owners often regard this behaviour as unacceptable. Indeed, in days gone by, horses would be fitted with various gadgets designed to make the maintenance of an erection extremely uncomfortable. Especially popular among the owners of funeral carriage horses, these devices took the form of barbs, harsh brushes and even electric-shock circuits. The motivation for horses to engage in this activity was thus matched by their owners' desire to prevent it. The effectiveness of the various widgets once available is indicated by the fact that over fifty different designs were patented for this job in the USA. Unfortunately, it was not until the 1980s that the scientific community recognised masturbation as a normal part of horse behaviour, thanks to an excellent paper by Sue McDonnell.

Question
Tasman is a six-year-old Fell gelding that I have owned since he was two. He was purchased locally from a private home that had owned him from weaning at ten months of age. He has become very attached to me, and loves it when I give him plenty of attention. I use him for leisure riding and competitive showing in mountain and moorland classes,

both in-hand and under saddle. Although Tasman is a bit naughty on the lunge – he tends to tow me around the paddock – his main problem is that he always protrudes his penis during in-hand show classes. For the last year this has happened every time we join the line-up, before the steward asks us to trot up individually. The first time he did this I was very embarrassed, as you can imagine, but no amount of distracting him (including offering him grass and mints) seems to make any difference. Why does he do this?

Answer
As a first step, I would ask your veterinary surgeon to check Tasman manually for any signs of his being a rig, and possibly even take a blood sample to check testosterone levels. If everything is unremarkable in these respects, I would suggest that the behaviour arose because you unconsciously gave Tasman positive reinforcement when he initially performed the behaviour.

Geldings protrude their penises prior to masturbation and urination. Neither of these possibilities seems relevant in Tasman's case because the instances of his doing it are so strongly circumstantial. It is of tremendous significance that he does it consistently only when being shown in-hand. He may genuinely have been preparing to urinate on that first occasion that caused you so much understandable embarrassment. Nowhere in any of the horsy textbooks does it tell one what to do in such a circumstance, and it was perfectly natural for you to have attempted to 'talk him out of it'. In keeping with up-to-date learning theories, I suggest that any fiddling, fussing or other attempts to distract him – for instance, by offering him grass – may actually have encouraged or rewarded him.

Now, it would appear that a number of cues serve to elicit the behaviour in Tasman. These probably include several things to do with attending a show, such as being washed and groomed, travelling, seeing you in your hacking-jacket, detecting your nervousness and entering the ring in-hand. Not surprisingly, whenever this sequence of events is repeated, it produces the same response from him. Furthermore, when he protrudes his penis you reliably react nervously and fuss over him, teasing him with grass and offering him mints, which unfortunately he views as a reward!

The way to extinguish this behaviour is to eliminate rewards altogether. In the first place, I would advise a temporary change of handler for the in-hand classes. Try to recruit someone who does not regard Tasman's success in the show ring as quite so important as you do, and ask him or her to ignore the problem when it presents itself. In the past, grooms have advocated the striking of any erect penis with a sharp stick. This is known to work, but it seems rather inhumane and, if painful enough to be effective, can elicit fear-based aggression when the horse learns to anticipate being struck.

Because horses have excellent memories, it will be at least two months before the behaviour starts to diminish through lack of reward. Eventually, however, it will abate. When you resume showing him, do so wearing a different jacket and perfume to avoid jogging his memory.

I would not advocate the use of any gadgets to modify his erection; Tasman really only dangles in the ring, so that would be where he would have to wear such a device. He might well soon learn that dangling only hurt when he was wearing the apparatus, and so might reserve his protrusions for times when you had chosen not to fit it.

Mounting (1)

Question
I have on loan an eight-year-old Connemara × TB gelding from an eventing family. Being so honest and bold, he has taught me a great deal about cross-country riding, but I have one reservation about his general enthusiasm: he always moves off as soon as I get on his back, which never gives me time to get myself sorted out and adjust my stirrup leathers and so forth. I find it very difficult to stop him because he just spins on the spot if I pull the reins. Why does he do this?

Answer
You have answered your own question to some extent by indicating that this gelding is a general enthusiast. He can't wait to get going, and you have allowed him to start the day's work without your giving him the OK. Now, we really don't want him to lose the zest that you describe. Instead,

what we should aim to do is teach him some rules – this is what has been omitted from the continuing education programme at his original home. But don't worry, it is never too late to reintroduce some fundamental manners. The other benefit, you will find, when he has lost this habit, is that he will be safer to ride.

At present, the cue for your horse to leave the yard is your getting on his back. As soon as he feels your weight in the saddle, he begins to walk away from the stable block. It is some time before you are settled enough to pull him up properly, and this delay stops him making the correct associations.

It is now a question of letting him know that the initial cue of your getting on his back means stand still. Find an area on your yard that provides an L-shaped barrier, such as a corner. Get a substantial mounting-block, a really large one that will present the horse with another barrier. With walls in front of and to the off-side of him, and a sturdy mounting-block to the near-side, your gelding will find premature departure impossible. If he is particularly fresh, you may have to ask a friend to help on the first few occasions by keeping him steady while you tighten his girth and so forth. When you are certain that *you* are ready to move off, give a verbal command to back up.

Eventually, you will be able to dispense with the inverted 'starting-box', but for an animal as forward-going as your gelding it remains good practice to persist with the requests for a few steps of rein-back before you start any exercise.

Mounting (2)

Mounting behaviour first appears in infancy, when many of the play manoeuvres used by colts involve mounting their peers and, to a lesser extent, their dams. I have also seen fillies mount their mothers, but this is far from common. If he is castrated as an experienced adult, a stallion may still mount mares for up to eighteen months, and some horses retain this behaviour for much longer – apparently through force of habit. For most male horses this does not apply because they are castrated when they are neither experienced nor adult.

Occasionally a mare may show stallion-like behaviour: for instance, by herding her companions with a snaking action and approaching them with an arched neck. Although this is not the norm for mares, it is similar to the behaviour of most female cattle when they are in season. It has been suggested that in cattle the function of the receptive female's willingness to be mounted by another female is to draw attention to the fact that she is ready for the bull. Since the recorded cases of this sort of behaviour in horses have sometimes involved uncooperative males – or, indeed, the absence of males – this may be a technique that has its origins in attempts to advertise the condition of a mare when her normal oestrous behaviour has failed to summon a willing male suitor.

Similar displays have been recorded in mares that have ovarian tumours which secrete excesses of testosterone into their circulation. So it is always worth having mares that show this sort of behaviour checked out by your veterinary surgeon, who will be able to clarify from an internal examination what it is that you are dealing with.

Question

My ten-year-old Hanoverian-Thoroughbred cross brood mare, Lulu, is a very easygoing character and has been part of the family for years. I retired her from dressage four years ago because of a suspensory ligament injury, and she has become more and more 'laid back' since then and never causes any bother. She is currently pregnant with her third foal and everything has been going swimmingly until last week, when I found her mounting my husband's hunter mare. She has since been spotted moving her three field-mates around the field and is behaving just like a stallion. Why is she doing this and what can I do to stop her?

Answer

I have encountered this intriguing history, although it is not common, on a number of occasions. The mares in question may show a broad spectrum of stallion-like behaviour, including trumpeting, herding and mounting.

It appears that many of these cases are directly related to hormone levels influenced by the foetus. This is because in horses, about halfway through pregnancy the gonads of the foetus – that is, its ovaries or testes – are larger than the maternal ovaries. If the unborn foal is male there is, therefore, the possibility of his production of male hormones outstripping his mother's production of female hormones. The resulting imbalance is capable of eliciting masculine behaviour in a female, and so many veterinarians believe that this is what is happening to most mares that exhibit these symptoms. Fortunately, the whole process is transient and requires no intervention as long as your mare's stallion-like behaviour does not precipitate injuries within the herd.

Question
I bought a Haflinger pony from a local sale three months ago. He was sold as a nine-year-old but I have my suspicions that he may be older. As a ride-and-drive pony he works brilliantly, but in the field with three Welsh cob mares his behaviour has aroused further suspicions because I am now concerned that he was not properly gelded. He was fine for the first month, but then I allowed a friend of mine to turn out her retired Thoroughbred gelding in the same field. The Haflinger became quite protective of the other horses and was always moving them away from the stranger. When one of the cobs came into season, he was spotted trying to mount her. The next day, he cornered the Thoroughbred and evidently managed to kick him through a barbed-wire fence. His voice seemed to change and, on one occasion, he bolted back to the field while being hacked out by my daughter, galloping across two busy main roads in the process. I think he is a rig. What steps can I take to confirm this?

Answer
It is interesting that you mention the doubts that you have about his age. The situation you are in is by no means uncommon for people who have bought through a sale ring. The expression, 'Let the buyer beware', is particularly appropriate when considering the exchange of horses in this way. The way most dealers work is that they allow for a number of bad buys each year. The volume of their turnover of horses means that they can afford to write off the occasional loss by sending those that cannot be resold back to the auction ring, and sometimes even to the abattoir. Private owners are not in this position. They tend to take

longer to identify horses with problems and therefore invest time, energy and patience in feeding and training them. On top of all this commitment there is also the likelihood of their developing an emotional attachment to the newcomer.

For all of these reasons the auction ring is not a good place for the amateur to buy horses. In a private sale a purchaser can request veterinary examinations and declarations of the absence of any behaviour problems. It is also possible to arrange short-term trials and contact with previous owners. Thus, the savings made by buying a horse at trade price are small compared with the peace of mind that other avenues offer.

Now to consider the possibility that he is a rig. It used to be said that the veterinary surgeon who gelded a colt that went on to display studdish behaviour must have left behind some of the epididymal tissue, which lies beside each testicle within the scrotum. This suggestion was based on the mistaken belief that the epididymis can produce testosterone. What seems more likely is that colts with partially descended testicles may have their epididymis inadvertently removed rather than the testicles themselves. As a colt matures, the epididymis descends into the scrotum in advance of the testicles and can therefore sometimes be the only structure obvious when the scrotum is opened at surgery.

There are some isolated incidents in which true geldings have actually achieved penetration. This is often put down to the gelding actually being a rig, although this cannot be established without the use of a blood sample. As far as we know, there are no disease processes in properly castrated male horses which cause an elevation of testosterone. However, testosterone, or analogous androgens, can be produced in sites other than the testicles – for instance, in the adrenal glands. Therefore, before surgery is attempted, a second set of tests can be applied if the vet is in any doubt as to the origin of the testosterone. Some equine behaviourists believe that riggish geldings can have similar male hormone levels to geldings that are completely free from amorous intentions. This is highly suggestive of a learned behaviour – for example, it can occasionally accompany late castration.

We know that a healthy libido is no indication of fertility, because the two factors are controlled by different hormones, albeit both produced in the testicles themselves.

N

Neighing

Question
I have a piebald cob mare called Donna who always neighs when she sees a herd of cattle when we go out on a ride. She never gets any response out of them, so I must say I feel rather sorry for her. She is kept in a field with lots of other horses and I don't think she is lonely. Why does she do it?

Answer
Some horses seem to recognise the difference between the shape of cattle and the shape of horses. They will therefore respond with fear if they are not familiar with cattle – this is a perfectly normal survival trait, known as neophobia. Other horses call to cattle in the same way as they would to horses, which suggests that, from a distance, these individuals do not make a clear distinction between the two species. This raises the whole debate about what horses can recognise. Anecdotes about their ability to see from a distance are plentiful. For example, it is claimed that Arabian horses used by nomads have correctly identified their owners from a distance of almost half a kilometre (500 yards). This phenomenal accuracy is very impressive, but it is not clear whether it was their owners' characteristic movements or their facial features that identified them.

Bernhard Grzimek showed that horses behave in response to a stylised two-dimensional image of a horse in the same way as they would towards a real horse – the approach and greeting were both similar. This may have been learned in infancy, when they imprinted on other horses simply as certain shapes that were safe to be with.

You will find that Donna does this only when she is a certain distance from the cattle. What is happening is that, quite simply, she is calling to them in the hope or belief that they are horses. Although she may eventually learn that these groups of large animals are not worth calling to, there are probably firmly established reasons for her making this mistake. It is interesting that Donna is piebald, because piebalds are most often the offspring of piebald dams, and have therefore imprinted on blocks of black and white hair during early development with the result that they seem to be ever-vigilant for this sort of pattern on any animal. The discrimination of colours has been reported many times by equine scientists. For example, there is a famous account of a feral stallion that selected only buckskin or dun mares for his harem. Unfortunately, the colour of his dam was not recorded, but his prejudice was sufficient to outweigh his innate motivation to reproduce with any receptive female.

Nervousness

We all know that some horses are more nervous than others, and because this is often related to their breeding we tend to regard the more finely bred individuals as especially stress-susceptible. Although in a mixed string of horses on a hack the Thoroughbred may be the most likely to spook at something lurking in the hedgerow, this does not necessarily mean that he is the most stressed. What we are talking about here is reactivity. Thoroughbreds have been selected to react quickly to stimuli; this is what allows them to leap out of a starting-stall while a cob would be wondering how he was supposed to graze in such a small space.

Researchers at Edinburgh University conducted an interesting experiment to illustrate the point that being responsive to certain sorts of stimuli does not necessarily amount to being stressed. They showed a bucketful of food to a variety of horses and ponies, but denied them immediate access to it – a process known (not surprisingly) as 'thwarting'. The behaviour and heart rates of the subjects were recorded during the procedure, and it was found that the most passive and apparently unperturbed animals, usually the ponies, had the greatest elevation in heart rate. On the other hand, the horses that created a foot-stamping rumpus because they could not get what they wanted when they wanted it showed less of a stress-related cardiac response. Further studies have shown that the more emotional horses are also the least able to learn. It is not clear if this is because they are less mentally agile or because they are struck by fear and therefore cannot complete the tests as quickly as better-adjusted individuals do.

The nervousness of some horses is not inbuilt, but results from prior experience. If, for instance, a horse has grown up being handled in a rough and unpredictable manner, he will learn to react defensively to a great variety of stimuli. This can make him extremely difficult to handle safely. At the other end of the spectrum are the horses that are nervous because they have grown up in relative isolation. These are the characters that never get exposed to traffic as youngsters and react with all due surprise when they are first ridden on the road. The aim of the enlightened horse keeper should be to find the middle ground that diminishes nervousness while enhancing trainability. This means spending plenty of time handling youngstock and habituating them to as many everyday stimuli as possible without arousing panic.

Nipping
Every time a horse nibbles at the grass under his nose he gets a reward for the behaviour. Unfortunately, the association between biting and the acquisition of a tasty snack leads to a degree of confusion in some horses. These are the notorious nippers.

Question
I have a seven-year-old Shetland pony, Ben, who used to belong to the landlord of our local pub. Ben was a beer-garden ornament and all the children used to play with him while their parents quenched their thirsts. He had been there three years when his habit of nipping got him into a spot of bother. He drew blood from a little boy's hand and was put on the 'transfer list'. The landlord felt it would be better for PR if Ben did not disappear completely, and that's how I came to be given him. I live just a little way down the road from the pub and lots of the pony's adoring public now loll over the fence to say hello to him. The only problem is that Ben is still nipping! Whenever hands are near his

mouth he is trying to nip them. This concerns me because my own children may be his next victims. I have been told to buy him a muzzle, but this idea doesn't really appeal to me. I would like to cure the habit rather than prevent it. What do you suggest for this sort of problem? Why are some ponies so keen to nip?

Answer
Ben has formed an association between human hands and food, because most of his young visitors bring him tasty snacks. His almost insatiable feeding urge, shared by so many other Shetlands, is aroused by the sight of humans. He wants food and knows that nine times out of ten it pays to show some interest. You see, Ben has learned that he can train humans to bring food to him – even the stupidest ones eventually realise that he will always walk away in disgust if the goodies do not flow thick and fast.

When he gets up close, Ben does not stop to consider whether the humans have come offering all manner of confection, or just plain affection. Being greedy, he immediately starts searching with his mouth. Hands are his first target because he often has only to nibble them to get his reward. In this way, numerous daily episodes of hand-feeding have reliably trained Ben, and many other ponies in pubs, zoos and pets' corners all over the world, that humans are glorified fast-food outlets.

Occasionally, nuzzlings and nippings are greeted with a clout across the face. This treatment does not teach the pony to stop biting, but simply to be very quick with his next nip. A variation on smash-and-grab, this blend of foraging and head-shyness is the quintessential equine snack-attack. The ponies that perfect this feeding strategy are those with a high motivation to feed and an excellent memory. Unfortunately, this rules out less than 1 per cent of the pony population! Almost any pony exposed daily to hand-held munchables will begin to lose his ability to discriminate between food and fingers, because biting either of these targets brings a flavoursome reward.

The most effective way to eliminate the behaviour is to break down the association between human hands and scrumptious snacks. In your situation, I would invest in some electric fencing, so that Ben can get within no more than a metre (yard) of his victims on the other side of the present fence line. They will still be able to see him, but any food they bring will have to be thrown on the ground beside him rather than hand-fed. It sounds as though Ben needs little in the way of supplementary feed but, obviously, when you feed him you too should discipline yourself to use a bucket.

Additionally, for guaranteed success in this extinction programme I recommend that you sacrifice an old pair of gloves. Coat them liberally with one of the proprietary taste-deterrents that are intended to reduce crib-biting and wood-chewing, and make sure that they are worn whenever you or your children say hello to Ben. This trick will help to confirm to him that his old fast-food outlets have an appalling new chef!

Nurture and nursing

In the months – sometimes years – that a foal spends with his dam, there is a constant exchange of care-eliciting behaviour and care-giving behaviour. Mares seem to be able to prompt a bout of suckling by approaching their foal or by standing and calling. The foal may run up to his mother in a characteristic manner that means that he needs her protection, or that he wants a drink.

When standing to nurse her foal, a mare helps out by resting the hindleg nearest to him, thereby making the closer of the two teats more accessible; in addition, the accompanying tilting of the whole udder towards the youngster also means that he can drink from both teats without having to change position. While the foal feeds, his dam will occasionally turn to check on him and possibly also to make sure that he hasn't brought any friends home to enjoy a free drink. When a second foal drinks from a mare he will often do so by nosing between her hindlegs, but even in this position he is not completely safe from detection and subsequent dispatch. At the end of a bout of nursing, the mare will often signal her intention to move away by racking the weight back on to the rested leg.

Although the foal would seem to be the only one of the maternal-infant pair to benefit opportunistically from their interaction, mares are thought to have mothering needs that are met by being able to nurse a foal. For instance, as mentioned earlier, if a mare's latest offspring dies or cannot suckle for some other reason she may well allow her previous foal to suckle, or even use her rank to steal the attentions of another mare's foal. Whether this arises because of inbuilt emotional needs or simply because it is the only way in which she can relieve uncomfortable pressure in her udder is unclear.

Experiments involving the serial separation of foals from their mothers suggest that the foal-mare attachment peaks one month after birth. In later life, foals that have been threatened – for example, by a dominant individual – will instinctively run to their dams even though they may have been weaned months, or even years, beforehand. This suggests that to their foals mares are a source of comfort, not just of milk. The allogrooming between foals and their dams has the same calming effect as it does between peers; this is demonstrated by reduced heart rates during mutual grooming.

O

Old age

Longevity in horses would appear to have a hereditary component. Certain bloodlines, especially of ponies, seem to be particularly long-lived. This characteristic is harder than most to select for in a breeding programme, since the animals with the genes to live a long time are identified as such only when they have gone beyond the age of reproduction. The relationship between longevity and behaviour may be that the wear and tear experienced by long-lived families may be less than in those that are shorter-lived. Conversely, this latter group may be more likely to take risks in life.

The ageing process in horses involves a number of physical changes, including the appearance of grey hairs. For grey horses this is particularly marked, because they can lose any dappling and become snowy white. Loss of pigment occurs all over the body in horses of all colours, but is especially noticeable around the eyes and mouth. It is difficult to see any evolutionary advantage to these colour changes – is it just one of those things? Older horses also get pits above their eyes, because the pad of subcutaneous fat, which normally fills this cavity and cushions the hinge of the lower jaw, tends to shrink.

The social changes which accompany ageing in horses are not kind, for the reason that reduced athleticism brings with it a lowered ability to manoeuvre around rivals. So in hierarchical challenges – over food, for instance – the older horse fares less well. This becomes most apparent in a domestic context when a newcomer is introduced to the herd. While established relations are not regularly disputed, the introduction of new animals always causes some adjustment in equine hierarchies. For these reasons, the lot of an aged animal on a dealer's yard is not a happy one.

P

Pawing

Pawing – which uses a similar action to gardeners hoeing – is a normal part of foraging behaviour in horses that are attempting to eat the roots of plants such as thistles or vetch. The behaviour is also seen when snow is on the ground, because the pawing action is the only effective way of revealing the meagre rations that may be hiding below the calorie-less canopy. Pawing is also seen during drought conditions when apparently dried-up drinking holes can be encouraged to provide a small pool of water by being deepened with the scraping action of a horse's hoof. Many horses paw in ponds and streams when they are hot, which has prompted some authors to suggest that this is an attempt to generate a cooling spray. Others are quick to point out that this could simply be an signal that an animal intends to roll. Another example of the use of the front hooves in this fashion is when sites are being tested for odours – for instance, when a stallion arrives at a dung pile.

These examples of pawing highlight particularly the importance of foreleg activity in certain feeding situations. All the circumstances described seem likely to involve a degree of frustration: as in the case of snow, which can be an obstacle to normal grazing activity. Indeed, it has been suggested that any situation that frustrates or, for that matter, excites a horse is capable of eliciting the same behaviour. Pawing can be viewed as feeding and comfort activity. It is also a signal of frustration to other horses. If you visit a stud where mares are hand-mated – that is, the stallion is led up to them rather than being allowed to run loose with them – you will also see pawing in any stallion held back from mounting – surely a source of frustration to any red-blooded male.

Other instances include pawing when tied up and when a ridden horse is asked to halt when it is keen to get going. Again, these are examples of frustration, but it is not clear whether they have their origins in feeding frustration. Some equine specialists would argue that food is so important to horses that anything that keeps them from it is sufficient to produce feeding-related frustration.

The presentation of concentrate food is certainly for many horses a highlight of the day. The excitement of anticipation is followed by ingestion, which satisfies the owner that the food is to the horse's liking. Enthusiastic eating has its origins in the social basis of equine life. The nearest equivalent in a feral context would be when a horse comes across a small, dense patch of sweet young grass: the law of the survival of the fittest dictates a strategy of eating it rapidly, before another horse does. The animal cannot take its time to savour the delicious meal. The excitement comes from the flavours that tend to characterise highly nutritious feedstuffs, while the frustration arises from the fact that the horse has evolved to dispatch the treasured find down its throat as soon as possible.

The problem for owners who try to prevent pawing is that, since it arises in feeding situations, it is often immediately rewarded. Horses that paw while eating are giving themselves a constant positive reinforcement, and it may even be that such a strong superstitious cause-and-effect association develops that they come to regard pawing as a sure means of getting the food they relish into their mouths. Thus it can become an obligatory part of the eating process.

Question
I have an eighteen-year-old Arab gelding called Magrob, who was gelded when he was ten years old. I keep him at grass but bring him in to groom and feed him twice a day. He is always waiting by the gate when I arrive, and if I am ever late he gets really stroppy with me. I can tell when he is agitated because the ground by the gateway is all chopped up and his legs are covered in mud. When he gets into the stable he wolfs his food down, with one foreleg – his right – continually pawing at the ground. I realise that he has made a habit of this pawing business and that I will never be able to stop it, but can you tell me why he does it? Do

you think his behaviour is related to the fact that he was gelded late in life? My vet says that he is likely to cause excessive wear and tear in the joints of his right leg – is this true?

Answer

Stallions are rather handy with their forefeet – that is, they are the most likely of all groups of horses to strike and paw. It is not clear whether Magrob's pawing behaviour developed when he was entire: it *could* be related to his life as a stallion, *or* to the time in his life after he was gelded. In my opinion this behaviour is always learned.

What you have described is yet another horse who just loves his food. This is an understandable trait because horses evolved on sparse seasonal food resources. They survived by being able to capitalise on food whenever it became available, and so to this day they enjoy feasting even in the absence of famine. The behaviour that Magrob exhibits has been learned in association with a food reward. From your letter, I would have to say that he has taught himself not only to paw at the ground but also to create a fuss at the gate. Your diligence in turning up and feeding him on schedule has reinforced the behaviour. While this is a credit to your devotion to Magrob and certainly not something for which you should feel guilty, the only way you could prevent him getting so wound up at feeding time would be to make his feeds less predictable.

So to avoid the food-related restlessness at the gate, try to give him his feed an hour or so early two or three times a week. Do not simply alternate, because Magrob may well begin to work out the pattern you have adopted. The other change you should make to his routine is in the way you feed him. As long as he is not going to be pestered by bullies in the same field, it would be useful to teach him that food can also be delivered to him in the paddock, at the opposite end to the gate. And when you feed him in this new site it is important that you do not enter the field through the gate. You may have to climb a fence, so that you arrive without having confirmed to him the relevance of the gateway by passing through it with a feed tub.

For a while Magrob may dash between the two sites, but eventually he will learn that the most economical strategy is to wait somewhere between the two – that is, in the centre of the field. The next step is to reduce the pawing. This is a behaviour that can be minimised by subduing the excitement that builds up before the feed, but it cannot be completely eliminated. Since there is an enormous learned component to the behaviour, unlearning or extinction would rely on removing the reward, in this case the food, every time Magrob paws at the ground. This is far from feasible, so all we can do is minimise the activity of his right leg by making it less easy for him to paw and eat at the same time. The feeding techniques that I have found useful include clipping the feed tub to the wall at ground level. Being so low, the tub flattens the horse's body posture and makes simultaneous pawing and eating more difficult than if the tub were at chest height. By clipping the tub to the wall you eliminate the chance of it going walkabout, which is a cue for many horses to start pawing. I do not recommend bolting the tub to the wall, since this makes it less safe and certainly less easy to clean. Feeding on concrete is another technique that helps to make pawing less comfortable.

Since Magrob has a strong motivation to consume his concentrate ration, you may try giving him something less palatable. If you can find a food with the same nutrient content but fewer grains or molasses, you will still nourish him but without getting him overexcited. Such rations tend to have a higher fibre content, which is more suitable for horses anyway.

Although I cannot comment on the force behind each pawing action, the possibility of uneven wear and tear on the right leg is a real danger with any repetitive concussive activity. So you would do well to heed your veterinary surgeon's warning and do something to minimise it.

Petting
Many owners like to show their affection for their horses by stroking their noses or patting their necks. Neck-patting is also a familiar punctuation mark in the schooling work-outs of many horses. But it seems that unless these interactions are linked to other, more directly rewarding, positive stimuli, they are unlikely to regard them as a big deal. The way to increase the reward value of a pat on the neck is to create an association with a tasty titbit. When the hand signal on

the neck is given at the same time as food (a primary reinforcer), the patting becomes what is known as a secondary reinforcer, and this is an ideal way of encouraging the horse to repeat the behaviour it has just performed.

Because, like most animals, horses have not evolved to give each other something for nothing, the relevance to them of petting and patting is questionable. Allogrooming (*see* Grooming, p. 143) is the word behaviourists use to describe mutual grooming – for instance, when a pair of horses engage in the familiar 'you scratch my back and I'll scratch yours' activity. It is usually initiated by the higher-ranking individual in the pair. Therefore, since scratching the neck has its basis in horse-to-horse behaviour, it can be a useful way of interacting with horses and of finding out how welcome one's favour actually is.

Among the most difficult areas for a horse to groom itself is the forehead, and other horses rarely stand and allow their flanks to be used as a scratching post for another horse's head. This is because, in such a T-shaped arrangement, they cannot be certain that the favour will be reciprocated. (The side-by-side stance, on the other hand, carries the benefit that each horse knows as soon as its effort is being wasted.) Consequently, rubbing the forehead is a straightforward reward to many horses. I tend to confine myself to this area when touching a horse's head affectionately. I believe the equine nose is not easily pleased when it comes to human attention, because the skin on the muzzle is especially sensitive and can be both tickled and abraded by the strokes of a human hand. I have also noticed that many horses find it very difficult to discriminate between the fun of having their heads rubbed all over by a human and the ecstasy of rubbing *their* heads all over humans! The horses that get intermittent head massages are the ones that rub their sweaty heads on you after a ride, sometimes hurting you with their bridle.

Pheromones

Pheromones are odours specifically designed to carry sexual signals such as the gender and reproductive status of the sender. Other features of these chemicals are that, to avoid confusion, they are unique to individuals, and that they can be detected in minute quantities. The study of equine pheromones is in its infancy, which is hardly surprising because these messenger chemicals are so difficult to isolate and identify. What makes our understanding of them even more elusive is the fact that we humans, with our poor sense of smell, are not very sensitive to them. So we have a poor appreciation of their importance in animal communication.

The role of pheromones in sexual behaviour has been highlighted in other species. For example, male moths can detect a receptive female from a distance of as much as six miles. It is useful to call to mind the imagery used in anti-perspirant adverts, in which the drive to be with the source of the scent, flying in the face of reason and the price of cut flowers, is portrayed as overpowering. The pheromones given off by a mare in season are capable of eliciting the same sort of departure from reason in stallions, who will literally walk through fences to get to their beckoning belle.

Preferences

Question
Ever since I bought my Welsh cob gelding, Caspar, as a weanling, he has taken hay from his hay net and dunked it in his water bucket before eating it. Although the stable tends to get slightly messy, I am not too concerned about the habit. However, my friend says this behaviour means that there could be something wrong with his kidneys. Is this true?

Answer
I have had horses with this behaviour trait and can assure you that all of them have been perfectly healthy. Perhaps a more fundamental question is: Why do horses prefer soaked hay? The simple answer is: Because it is more natural for horses to consume grass that is succulent rather than dried. Being already in solution, the flavours are more readily available to the taste buds. Anyone who has chewed on liquorice roots will confirm that dried plant matter tastes of very little until it is moistened by saliva to release water-soluble sugars and flavoursome compounds. Having said that, I must add that there are also some horses that prefer dried hay. It all seems to boil down to personal preference.

The horses that do not soak their hay in this way may be

less motivated to adjust the water content of their forage ration. Alternatively, they may be unable to work out how to do it. Therefore, far from regarding dunking as a 'habit', I would encourage you to view it as an indication of Caspar's problem-solving ability.

To be fair to Caspar, I would say that he is simply exercising choice. Horses that behave in this way are actually working to improve their environment in the same way that horses suffering from the painful muscle condition azoturia sometimes build mounds in their bedding. It is believed that the muscles of the back are among the worst affected by this dreadful condition, so for azoturia patients the mounds are useful as perches that help to relieve back pain. Clearly, compared with this emergency strategy, dunking to moisten dried fibre is far less alarming. Just because your cob seems to demand more liquid in his diet does not mean that he is having any trouble conserving water. So ignore your friend's diagnosis and relax in the knowledge that Caspar is a clever cob.

You will notice that he doesn't dunk when you offer him freshly cut grass, or indeed hay that has been soaked for an hour or so. And there are certain health reasons that make it generally better to feed soaked hay – one does not have to wait for one's horse to start coughing before he can benefit from this management practice! The best way to eliminate the behaviour is to regard it as a subtle hint and start pre-dunking your horse's hay biscuits.

Question
I have a four-year-old Appaloosa gelding that I have hopes of competing with when he is fully mature. His bloodlines suggest that he may be useful as an endurance horse, and he is already showing signs of having the right temperament for that job. He loves work and can't wait to get going whenever we leave the yard for a ride. I've also noticed that he tends to speed up every time I ask him to go uphill. Why does this happen?

Answer
Many owners report that their horses would rather go uphill than down, and there are a number of reasons for this preference. Firstly, horses tend to carry 60 per cent of their

body weight on the forehand (front legs) and so find travelling downhill less easy. This is confirmed by the increased care that they take when travelling downhill. It has also been suggested that when they travel uphill they can more easily navigate a path than when the ground is falling away from them on a descent. This theory has yet to be confirmed by scientific publication but it certainly seems to make sense when you consider that a horse's so-called blind spot is right under his nose!

The other innate reason that horses prefer going uphill to downhill is because of their evolutionary origin as a prey species. This dictates that they should always move in a way that lends some strategic advantage, should the need to flee arise. The strategic advantage of running uphill when in danger is that it affords a better view of what is going on and reduces the risk of being pounced upon. Most prey species share this tendency, and for this reason races and ramps in sheep- and pig-handling facilities always tend to be designed to include climbs rather than descents.

Riders, too, develop a preference for reserving fast work for uphill travel because it is safer and more comfortable for them than when they attempt the same downhill. Thus, the tendency for horses to pick up speed whenever a hill presents itself can be a conditioned response. Furthermore, the lower parts of their legs are far less likely to suffer wear and tear if they are spared the rigours of fast downhill work, which increases the forces acting on their tendons and ligaments.

Pulling

Horses pull on the reins because they derive some reward or benefit from doing so. In the case of a horse that seizes the bit and extends his neck, thus pulling the reins through the rider's hands, the reward is that the contact is much looser. For the horse that is keen to get going, this reduction in contact has the advantage that the pace cannot easily be slowed down. Horses that like to jog on their way home often try this tactic, because it means that they can get where they want to be faster. Similarly, horses that pull when put into fast work do so because they thereby gain the advantage of being able to set their own pace.

The other advantage of pulling the reins out of the rider's

hands is that the horse can make himself more comfortable. Many horses find that being ridden on the bit (in other words, with the line of the head at right angles to the ground) is far from comfortable if it has to be held for any length of time. When the head is in the required position, the absence of pressure on the reins is the horse's reward. While this posture has its origins in display behaviour among loose horses, it is rarely maintained continually through changes in pace and direction. Furthermore, even when loose, some horses never assume this head position. This may be because they are simply not built to adopt it easily or because they experience a degree of neck or back pain that makes it uncomfortable. Consequently, to insist on a regimented relationship between head and neck in every ridden horse is far from realistic. Every good dressage rider will acknowledge that some horses are easier to 'get into an outline' than others. This is not because they have a greater desire to please their owners, but because the posture is easier for them to achieve.

Question
I have owned Frenchie my ten-year-old Thoroughbred since he was five. He had a reasonably successful racing career before I bought him, and I can see why: he's always in a rush to get going at the start of a hack and hates standing still. I enjoy hunter-chasing with him because, for me, it is one discipline that doesn't require too much in the steering and brakes department, neither of which are Frenchie's forte. He persistently hangs on to the bit on the off-side rein and, as a result, my biceps are really rather enormous on that side. I've spent hours schooling him on the flat but he forgets all his manners when we pick up speed. I realise that a hard mouth is irredeemable, but is there anything I can do to redress the balance between the left and right reins?

Answer
Reasons for pulling to the left or right are similar to those that underlie the horse's understanding of comfort and reward. The terms 'hollow', 'stiff' and 'resistant' are applied to horses that do not work with an equal pressure on both reins. The problem is compounded by the fact that most

humans are either left- or right-handed, which means that they tend to use unequal forces with their hands; and, furthermore, their balance is also one-sided. The art of good equitation lies in an ability to master these imbalances.

From your letter, it is not clear whether you regard your own built-up muscles as desirable or embarrassing, but the implications for Frenchie can never be good! He will doubtless show more tone in muscle groups on the right of his neck, and if this imbalance is marked he will even have trouble in stretching his neck properly. Therefore, being especially hardened in the right-hand side of his mouth is likely to be the least of his problems.

A hard mouth is one that has become insensitive to pressure on the bit as a result of continual overstimulation – for example, because the horse has had riders who have always pulled on the reins in search of the elusive concept known as 'contact'. Anyone who has carried a rucksack for any length of time will confirm that continual pressure leads to discomfort and eventually numbness, through reduced blood supply if nothing else.

From my own research I deduce that horses are certainly capable of being left- or right-handed – that is, they can show a preference for straying in one direction rather than the other. It is up to us to make appropriate allowances for one-sidedness, and this is why experienced trainers make sure they establish the extent and direction of any stiffness within minutes of starting work with a new horse. Furthermore, always being led from one side, traditionally the horse's left-hand side (near-side), tends to make left-handed horses even more sensitive to information arising on that side of their bodies.

Since pain and discomfort can culminate in numbness, insensitivity to pressure from the bit, the rein and even the leg can result. The origins of unilateral pain can include oral abnormalities such as sharp spurs on molar teeth, the presence of wolf-teeth, and cuts, ulcers and tooth-root abscesses. Neck pain can arise from a previous fall and even from something as well intentioned as an injection. For this reason, most vets avoid the neck as an injection site because the resultant stiffness, though temporary, can make a dressage animal less supple and a jumper far less agile, thereby costing them several places in competition.

The other point to bear in mind is that it takes two to pull. This expression is an old one, but it can bear repetition because so many riders dismount complaining of having their arms pulled out of their sockets! When the forces running along the reins exceed those generated by the contact between hand and mouth a nagging process is likely to develop, with the rider applying pressure on the tongue and the horse learning to ignore it. What I regard as bizarre is that it always seems to be the horse that is described as the puller; we seem to forget that he is pulling against an opposing force – that applied by the rider.

The way to remedy numbness on one side of the mouth is simply to give it a rest by easing the tension applied to that rein. And the way to remedy stiffness on one side of the neck is to get it moving. Thus, bending exercises which encourage the horse to flex his neck in the desired direction are invaluable for both problems. The other school movement to use is shoulder-in and turns on the forehand, both of which help to generally loosen the lateral musculature. Finally, I recommend the use of a finer rein on the right. This will help to remind you that you should always be concentrating on giving to that side as much as possible.

Pushing

Question

For the last four years, I have owned an Irish Draught × TB called Stanley. He is a heavyweight show hunter and also does a bit of unaffiliated show-jumping. He is completely bomb-proof on the roads and is a real gentleman in the box, but he has one annoying habit that I find quite frightening. Whenever I pull his mane – for instance, to smarten him up for the show season – he gets really het up, and after I have tugged at it three or four times he tries to tread on me and crush me against the nearest wall. If I persist he starts throwing his head around and squealing. I've tried twitching him, but he seems to be able to fight that. Last week I even tried pulling his mane while sitting on his back, but he spun around and reared so I had to give up on that idea. I'm reluctant to have to ask the vet to sedate him for this job, so I was wondering if you could suggest where he got this trick from and how I may be able to stop him doing it?

Answer

The main reason for Stanley's unwelcome behaviour is the pain that this procedure tends to involve. It seems to have crept into the folklore of horse-keeping that manes have no feeling. This is probably because novice riders are encouraged to hold on to the hairs on the neck when they feel nervous. Grabbing such a hearty handful of mane that it could not possibly be pulled off the horse's neck is one thing, but taking several strands at a time with the express intention of pulling them out is quite another. Many horses become resentful of this part of the grooming process, and adopt defensive strategies as soon as they realise that for the ensuing thirty minutes they are to be slowly scalped. Stanley is one of those horses, and his memory of the discomfort of mane-pulling prompts him to take effective steps to prevent it happening.

Given that he has only to stop you tugging for a few moments to get his reward, it is hardly surprising that he regards the hard-shoe shuffle as the most effective step he can take. He knows that you have to take a sharp intake of breath, uncross your eyes and reposition him at some distance from you before you can resume the pulling process, and this respite makes crushing well worth while. I will discuss strategies that you can use to groom Stanley more safely, but first I want to minimise the extent to which he regards you as a pain in the neck.

If you need to pull hairs it is certainly important, on humane grounds, to do so after exercise. When the pores of the skin open to allow Stanley's body to cool down, his hair follicles are less tightly secured and can therefore be pulled with less twingeing of nerve endings. In the same vein, it really is very important with horses as sensitive as yours to discipline yourself to avoid the temptation to remove tresses in one fell swoop. Just confine your daily pulling to the three or four tugs that Stanley will tolerate, and then give him a reward. Do not reward him if he has moved you in the direction of the wall! People who say that it is spineless to pander to a horse's feelings in this way have probably not had half the hairs on their heads determinedly pulled out by a friend twice a year.

It is perfectly acceptable to remove small numbers of hairs while you are on Stanley's back after exercise, and you can position a mane comb on the fence post at the entrance to the yard to remind you to do so every time you return home. Generally, when you are grooming Stanley, it would be advisable to use a single post rather than a rail or a ring on the wall, because this will eliminate any fixed barrier against which he could push you. My other safety tip is primarily intended to spare your toes from that characteristic crunching sensation. The idea is simply to get your feet off ground level to a height that does not accommodate horse hooves. A plastic milk crate will suffice for this job, but it has to be moved regularly as you groom the different parts of the horse. As an alternative, old railway sleepers placed alongside him will provide the ideal platform for grooming and mane-pulling.

R

Rank

A distinction between dominance-subordinance and tolerance-attachment appears to be gaining favour. Essentially, this novel theory of equine rank suggests that the degree of tolerance applied to a herd member by the highest-ranking individual generates a sub-system of preferred status within the dominance system. By increasing the length of time during which a favoured subordinate is allowed access to a resource, this sub-system modifies the influence of social structure on interactions and feeding. The herd has evolved to enhance the protection of individuals against predators, and its cohesion is maintained by a variety of mutually beneficial behaviours such as allogrooming and tail-to-tail fly-swatting.

Agonistic behaviour is dependent on herd size: in small groups a linear dominance hierarchy is usual, while triangular and more complicated relationships can develop in large herds. Once a dominance hierarchy has been established, aggression becomes more ritualised. The use of the term 'dominance' is somewhat controversial, since some authors highlight avoidance behaviour on the part of subordinates as the main activity necessary for the maintenance of the order. In view of this, it has been argued that the 'avoidance order' is a better measure of the social system than the 'aggression order'.

The determination that horses often show when they are getting to know one another is a measure of the importance they attach to social organisation and rank. The quest for higher ground in the equine social ratings is far more important to horses than are the rather sad wranglings between humans to those involved. Keeping up with the proverbial Joneses occupies the minds of humans who have nothing more important to worry about. For horses, on the other hand, rank can be literally a matter of life and death. In a domestic environment we try to provide adequate food and water for our equine charges, and it is easy for us to forget the importance of these resources when they are limited. Free-ranging horses are usually familiar with the seasonal disappearance of food sources, and it is at these times of relative paucity that rank can mean the difference between surviving and perishing. The horse that demands access to the best of what food is available is less likely to suffer illness and is also the least likely to be lethargic when escaping a potential predator. The success of the genes within each horse depends on that horse being able to access resources and breed a future generation of fighting-fit foals.

Rank is influenced by many factors, such as prior fighting experience, skill, strength and stamina. Therefore, it is worth considering all of these when watching horses as they interact in a group. Other factors that one might otherwise overlook include the rank of the dam, because to some extent rank can be passed through generations. It is difficult to be certain whether this transmission is due to learning successful strategies, or to the bloodlines having greater inherent motivation to secure key resources. Given that most hierarchies are established in relation to food resources, behavioural scientists may rank a pair of horses by presenting them with a bucket of food and recording who ends up with it.

The suggestion that stallions lead a herd by domination is now regarded as debatable. The snaking motion that a stallion displays with his head and neck in order to move mares and foals as a group does not relate to rank; since it is used to enhance the safety and viability of the group, energy would be wasted if a hierarchical dispute were entered into every time a stallion tried to move a high-ranking mare out of danger. The time of the year has an effect on the status of stallions. Being in season or having a foal at foot tends to elevate the rank of mares – which can have important repercussions when owners reintroduce a mare into an established group. If she has a foal at foot her rank will be elevated from her previous status in the group, and more disputes than might be expected will arise before resolution is reached.

Another factor that seems to influence rank is the length of time that a horse has spent in the group. This seems to have something to do with the establishment of mutually beneficial coalitions that allow bonded pairs to collaborate in disputes against a third party. The phenomenon gives rise to the triangular relationship that we occasionally see when we examine mature equine dominance hierarchies. In this case, the rank of one band member relative to another is dependent on the presence of a third. Perhaps this is why band fission is a possible consequence of the death or removal of a band member.

Because there are so many factors at play, and because no single variable can outweigh the others when we are determining rank in a fresh grouping of horses, there are often surprises in store, and changes occur that may upset owners. Horses have no regard for 'fair play' or 'justice'; they do what they have to in order to ensure that their genes survive. They never adopt policies that are 'good for the species'. And the concept of bullying is a human one. Since competitive performance bears little relation to hierarchical position, owners become very frustrated when the boss of their herd is neither the most valuable nor the best athlete. When the boss puts 'better' horses in their place with kicks and bites that affect success in competition, owners' frustration can even turn to anger.

Question
I keep two British spotted ponies at a local riding school on a part-livery basis. They seem to want to be together all the time but I regularly find them fighting over food, so I have trouble deciding which one is the boss. The owner of the school is a horse dealer, so there are always new horses coming on to the yard and these seem to upset all of the resident horses. How can I determine which of my two ponies is the boss? I have been told that knowing about their rank is important because I need to decide which I should feed first at night. Is this true?

The dominant horse always ends up with the bucket.

Answer

For a human observer to work out the rankings in a group of horses, he or she must spend a lot of time watching them and be in a position to comment on the dominance relationship between every pair of horses in the group. As already mentioned, when research scientists test for dominance by giving two horses one bucket of food, it is the dominant horse that always ends up with the bucket. Naturally, this test can generate all sorts of disputes, so most experiments are conducted with a fence that minimises injury by separating the two participants from the bucket holder. If you were able to do this sort of test with your two ponies, the result that you would emerge with could only be used with caution, however. All that you would have established would be which one of the ponies is dominant in an isolated food-related hierarchy. What you would still have to consider is the possibility of a coalition existing that involved the subordinate pony and a third horse whose presence could effectively demote the original boss. The other important factor to remember is that hierarchies involving resources other than food – for instance, access to water or a new herd member – might have a different outcome.

This brings me to another interesting point that you raise: the question of ranks being in a constant state of flux as a result of the introduction of new herd members and the removal of established ones. You will have noticed the turmoil that develops every time the horse dealer brings another horse home. The cuts and bruises on the horses are matched by the skid marks in the paddock. The social structure of horse communities is designed to withstand the occasional sort-out, if harmony is allowed to reign for some time afterwards. This is never going to be possible on a busy dealer's yard, and so from a welfare point of view the situation that you describe is far from ideal.

As far as the order of feeding is concerned, I suspect that whoever suggested that this was important for your horses was overinterpreting similar guidelines concerning the feeding of other species in a ranked group. The order in which dogs are fed is indeed of great importance, but this is chiefly because they are pack hunters and hence communal eaters with the need to split the spoils of a hunt in accordance with their hierarchy. Horses, on the other hand, have evolved to eat as a disseminated group, which is why they are better fed any concentrate rations in separate stables or at least out of the range of others. It would be inadvisable and even rather dangerous to feed your ponies in the field situation that you describe.

Rearing

In feral contexts, horses (especially stallions) rear when they are fighting and when they have to confront something aversive. Rearing has the advantage of at once raising the horse's height, which both improves his viewpoint and makes him more fearsome. It also puts a good space between him and the given adversary or object of fear. It is therefore the ideal strategy for self-defence because it increases the horse's weaponry and at the same time saves his forelegs from becoming trapped. The sort of trigger that causes rearing in the wild is the sudden appearance of a small carnivore at the muzzle of a grazing horse.

Question

I have a three-year-old Thoroughbred × Irish Draught colt that I have been showing in-hand for the last twelve months. He used to be the quietest character on the local in-hand circuit, but he has been rearing with increasing regularity over the last six weeks or so. The problem is so bad that I am thinking about having him castrated. Why has this suddenly become such a problem?

Answer

Very often a youngster rears for the first time through sheer *joie de vivre*. The important thing for the handler is to respond correctly to this behaviour. If the horse is hit when he comes within striking distance, he will soon learn to associate coming down to the ground with pain and decide to stand up on his hindlegs for as long as possible. Furthermore, if he develops a fear of you as a result of this sort of approach and perceives you as an adversary rather than a companion, he will be more likely to enter into combat with you as he matures.

Play in feral horses of this age becomes increasingly boisterous, so you should aim to reappraise the relationship that you have with your colt. Many home-bred youngsters that have been the apple of their owners' eye develop disappointingly aggressive behaviour at this point in their lives. I can never recommend that novices play rough games with youngstock in a bid to bond with them. The dangers of these interactions being misinterpreted by a youngster, especially one that may lack the appropriate equine company, are too great. This is by no means an invitation to abandon early handling – which has been shown to enhance learning ability – but merely to limit it to simple handling and not to allow it to spiral into familiarity. The breaking of bonds between pairs of foals that have grown up together tends to occur with the onset of sexual maturity, and most youngstock are likely to have a sort-out in this adolescent period. The important thing for the breeder to remember is that this is the time when ranks between peers are redefined and when, in any interaction, humans should be seen to dominate. For instance, when given food a young horse should never be allowed to threaten the humans around him, even by simply pulling faces. The tendency is to dismiss this behaviour as mildly amusing, but from the horse's point of view the sight of a human leaving a bowl of feed for him after a facial threat is a sign of submissive, not dismissive, behaviour.

The point at which the young horse starts to throw his weight around is precisely when you should begin a serious education programme; the alternative is that he will train himself. The important aspect for you to concentrate on is keeping control: if your colt learns that you are frightened of him, or that he can tow you around, your task in regaining some authority will become monumental.

I would regard his repeated rearing very seriously, for the reasons I have given. You must regain control as soon as possible after each rear. The chances are that he is rearing because he does not want to go the way you want him to – that is, because he expects something in that direction to be aversive. This may simply be because to advance is to distance himself further from his companions, or because there is something directly unappealing in front of him. Either way, you cannot afford to let him think that rearing is a stunt that he can pull in order to get his own way. It is therefore imperative that, as soon as he touches the ground with his front feet, you send him forward in the direction that has caused the baulking. This is why you should always carry a schooling-whip with a young animal; it can be vital as an aid to send him forward and will also help to prevent him landing on you.

Finally, I would encourage you to consider the possible effects of the tack you use on your colt. When handling stallions and youngstock, many people use a running chain from the off-side ring of the snaffle-bit through the near-side. This acts as the chain version of a slip-knot and tightens rapidly when the horse pulls forward. It has found favour because it offers so much control, should the horse lurch forward. However, every time he pulls he feels considerable pain all around the lower jaw. Should he pull *back*, the noose will slide forward and sit in an unfamiliar position, and the first time this happens he may respond with surprise. If his surprise is acute he will rear, and as the noose is tightened around his teeth things will rapidly go from bad to worse. For this reason, I feel that running chains should be used with tremendous discretion.

If you feel that you will be unable to regain complete control by being more authoritative with him, then castration may be the only option.

Refusal to jump

Horses have evolved to avoid obstacles by circumventing them, rather than taking the more risky option of jumping them. With familiar territory the risks are not such an issue, but every time a novice horse approaches a fence or a ditch years of evolution are telling him to take great care. The ground on the landing side could be treacherously boggy or, worse still, could be harbouring a hungry predator.

Question

When I bought my British Warm-blood as a three-year-old colt I had visions of competing in all sorts of show-jumping and combined training competitions, but things have not worked out. He is five now and still will not jump a stick. When my riding instructor decided to loose-school him over jumps recently, he seemed quite happy to jump almost anything. It is so disappointing to think that he won't do the same with someone riding him. Can you suggest what is going on?'

Answer

Without seeing your horse approach a fence with and without you on his back, it is difficult for me to make any informed judgements on his own particular behaviour. Instead, I would like to offer some general points that should be addressed when one is presented with a problem of this sort.

The first question, with a show-jumper that refuses, has to be: Is he capable of doing what is asked of him? It would appear that your horse is agile enough to jump without you on his back, because he can tackle the jumps in the loose-school situation. Most horses cope very well with humans of average weight, so the extra weight he has to carry when you are on board is unlikely to make a critical difference to his ability over novice-sized fences. What is always worth checking is the way the saddle rests on his back *when carrying a rider,* since pinching and rocking may make jumping and, more especially, landing prohibitively uncomfortable for the unfortunate horse.

The second question is: Does the horse know what is required of him? The important point to remember here is that horses are *not* born natural jumpers but, rather, instinctively avoid hazards in their path. Jumping has to be *taught* with generous use of wings and, where possible, jumping-lanes. The idea behind training a horse to jump with the help of directional barriers is that he will develop an association that links the sight of a jump with the sense that clearing it is the best strategy to adopt in order to get beyond it. This concept of 'errorless learning' has also found favour in the world of dog-training, with the enthusiastic campaigning of my colleague in the Association of Pet Behaviour Counsellors, John Fisher. The basic point to remember for errorless learning is that if refusing and running out are presented as possible options in your horse's behavioural repertoire, then he will definitely use them. Many horses are actively taught to refuse by riders who lose impulsion one or two strides from the fence.

Finally, in order to understand horses that are not keen to jump it pays to consider the possible reasons for their lack of appropriate motivation. The positive rewards that your horse expects for doing what you want are outweighed by the negative expectations associated with doing it. For instance, if in the past for some reason he has been jabbed in the mouth every time he has jumped a fence, his positive associations with travelling at speed or pleasing you are often not going to be sufficient to overcome his fear. Similarly, if we consider the routine thrashings that some horses get every time they refuse, it is clear that there is something about the jump that is even more aversive than the predictable pain of being hit. It is vital for owners to identify and eliminate any aversive aspect to the jump itself.

The other strategy to consider is one that develops the horse's positive motivation to jump. Praising him is certainly worth while, but engineering events so that he actually enjoys jumping seems to be the real key. For instance, the prospect of joining companions on the far side of the fence can be used as an appealing goal for him to head for. Using school-masters or lead-horses in this way is an excellent and sadly underexploited training aid.

To summarise: the reasons for and against jumping are weighed up in your horse's mind every time he is presented with a jump. Until you know him well enough to appreciate his key pros and cons you will never be able effectively to resolve a refusal problem.

Refusal to load
As with jumping fences, there are plenty of reasons why horses, as a species that has evolved in open spaces with wide views, should dislike the perils of enclosed travel. Being trapped in a dark, noisy hole is hardly something we can expect them to relish!

It is unfortunate that few people who drive horse-transporters have taken the time to stand in the back of a trailer as it is driven around a field. Horse-trailers do not just rock from side to side – they lurch forward and back, throwing most horses off balance. This is believed to be one of the main reasons why trailers that tow them facing forwards are especially disliked by some horses. Essentially, this is because the weight distribution over a horse's body tends to make him better at bracing himself against forward than against backward propulsion; he can enhance his bracing capabilities by leaning against the trailer's ramp.

The virtues of backward-facing travel for horses are being acknowledged by equine scientists all over the globe – although the horse world appears as usual to be so bogged down in its sense of tradition that designers of horse-boxes have yet to feel the demand for this novel design. Loading problems will diminish only when horses have access to forms of transit that are less aversive.

Question
I have a middle-weight show cob called Stubbs, who is rising ten. He has competed successfully at county level for the last two years and is tipped for the top in the coming season. He has one terrible drawback, however, which could very easily affect his show career: he can be very difficult to load. Many times this summer the sun has set before he has deigned to get aboard. I have never yet had to leave him at a show ground, but I must admit to having considered that it would be an excellent final solution on a number of occasions. When he sees the ramp of the box he starts to

shuffle backwards, and then when he gets really close he rears to the left or the right and scuttles away. To my knowledge he has never had an accident in the box and scarcely gets sweated up, so why does he have this dislike for loading?

Answer
The majority of horses that do not load well are either frightened of the box and of the associated journey, or they are conditioned to be fearful of loading because of their previous experience of aversive loading regimes. I still see the use of whips and yard-brushes advocated as the easy answer to getting horses into boxes. These may work in the short term, but on the whole they make most horses more afraid of the whole loading process than they need to be. In fact, the only place for such methods is in an emergency, such as needing to get to the vet for urgent surgery.

Members of the Equine Behaviour Study Circle (details of which appear in the Appendix) recently came up with several tips that improve matters in the short term. Bear these in mind for long-term training sessions, too, so that Stubbs's evasion tactics are made as fruitless as possible:

1 Fit a standing martingale to the head-collar and then to a surcingle, to stop him throwing up his head.
2 Halve his chances of escaping to the sides by putting the box next to a wall or in a gateway.
3 Place his feet on the ramp if he is so naive that he does not know that he can do so.
4 Ask two helpers to hold a lunge line several metres (yards) behind him. This should be used to prevent reversal, rather than as a primary means of pushing him into the box. Remember that pushing a fearful animal towards something it is scared of is rather like shoving a non-swimmer into the deep end of a pool – it does nothing to overcome the fear.
5 Avoid transporting him in a traditional trailer that makes him face forward – bigger wagons are much better – and drive as carefully as possible so that he doesn't get scared.
6 Remember that the more hungry Stubbs is, the more likely he is to overcome his fear and enter the box for food reward. So, give him as little as possible to eat at the show itself.

In the long term, the best tried and tested method involves habituation and counter-conditioning, but it requires considerable devotion. In this programme you provide all feeds in the box, and repeat the loading procedure but without any subsequent travel. Between classes at a show is the ideal time to devote to the pursuit of excellence in ramp-climbing! Sadly, very few owners capitalise on the wealth of helping hands and co-operative lead-horses available at most shows because embarrassment seems to get the better of them. Instead, they prefer to wait until the end of the day before recruiting ever-more frustrated volunteers, each with his own fool-proof gimmick.

Rolling

Question
I have a five-year-old grey Arab that my next-door neighbour bred. He is a real character and seems to know exactly what is expected of him when ridden. I am showing him just in ridden Arab classes at the moment, but would like to do endurance trials when he is old enough. I'm certain that getting him ready for a long-distance ride will be easier than preparing him for a show. The problem I have is that every time I give him a bath he rolls. This means that I can never wash him the day before a show because the following morning he is caked in filth. Do you know of an easy way round this?

Answer
Most people with greys do acknowledge the possibility of having to give them a bath on the morning of a show for the very reasons you have given. Even if you stable him overnight, you have the problem of faecal staining which is often worse than good old mud. If you could give him a bath early on the previous day and then place him in his box with a bed of clean sand or fresh shavings, he might well use that to dry off. Then you could turn him out in the field overnight with less chance of him rolling.

A thorough washing allows water (and even suds) to find its way into nooks and crannies that would remain dry even in a downpour – a far more natural way for a horse to get wet. So the feel of the water as it courses through his coat and the subsequent sensation of it drying in a rather unsettled fashion, especially if towelled over, is sufficient to prompt a thorough rolling. The intention seems not so much to get rid of the unwanted odours associated with the recent scrubbing as to get comfortable.

In feral horses, rolling is a social grooming process and also a means of drying off after the herd has been stirred into fast movement on a hot day. You will have already noticed how many horses love a good roll after a ride or drive. It is thought that rolling also has ritual significance for groups of horses, the members of which will take turns to wriggle in the dusty delights of a favoured site.

Question
Ever since I bought my Cleveland Bay × TB gelding Jesse as a four-year-old three years ago, I have had problems with him in water. He has a passion for rolling in ponds and streams, usually after the first half of the ride, but never waits for me to get off and remove the saddle before he gets down to indulge himself. Fortunately, he gives me plenty of warning by grunting a bit before his knees and hocks start to crumple beneath him, so I can kick my stirrups and jump off quickly enough to avoid being crushed. As you can probably imagine he is a very big lad, and I wouldn't want to get stuck underneath him! He has already broken the trees of two saddles and the insurance company does not cover me against that sort of damage, so the expense is as much of a problem as the danger. Can you suggest why he does this and how I can get some resolution?

Answer
It may be the feel of soft ground under foot rather than the water in a pond or stream that elicits in so many horses the desire to roll. It is an innate behaviour used by some feral horses to cool down, and this may explain why you experience most of your problems in the second half of the ride, when Jesse has warmed up. Furthermore, many horses will have an occasional roll *after* a ride, and the main reason for this seems to be the accumulated moisture under the saddle area after a healthy work-out, which provokes the sort of drying behaviour seen in feral animals. However, horses

that insist on rolling after *every* ride are a possible cause for concern.

In the short term, one can overcome the water-related problem by the firm use of leg aids as you travel through water but, given the predictability of Jesse's behaviour – his tendency to roll religiously during every ride – I would encourage you to stop riding him until you have had his back and saddle examined. I find that horses wearing rather uncomfortable saddles which reduce the blood supply in areas of tissue and skin on their backs tend to be the most likely sufferers. These deprived back areas become very itchy or painful every time the saddle is used for any length of time, and the only tactic for relieving an itch of this magnitude is to roll. Similar situations arise with horses in irregular work, whose backs have not habituated to the pressure of bearing a saddle. This speaks of the discomfort of a saddle for a horse in soft condition and of the need to alleviate an under-the-saddle itch, to which the safety of the rider takes second place.

Take the time to examine the hairs on your horse's back next time you remove the saddle. See if any areas are being worn unevenly, or if there are patches where the hair is being forced 'against the grain' by the movement of the saddle. Also, it is worth looking at the numnah (saddle pad) to spot areas of particular wear and especially heavy soiling that can point to excessive pressure. Checking the saddle itself is certainly not a job for an amateur, since considerable experience is required to discern the differences between incorrect stuffing, old stuffing and perfect stuffing. The most high-tech saddlers now have access to computer-imaging methods that identify and grade any pressure points under a saddle. Even without this sort of equipment, your saddler will be able to give you his opinion on whether the saddle requires attention or whether perhaps you should invest in a gel-pad numnah.

S

Shying

Feral horses shy to avoid being caught by potential predators – they run first and then ask questions. This is why shying away from an object regarded as threatening is rarely preceded by exploration of the possible risks involved.

An owner may detect that his or her horse is more likely to shy from one side than from the other. Visual defects in one eye are often blamed for the onset of spooking and shying from the side concerned, but on subsequent veterinary investigation are not a common finding. If there are problems with the eyes, a veterinary surgeon will be able to give you an assessment of their effects on your horse's perception of the world. The important point to remember is that the complete loss of sight in one eye is a handicap that most horses rapidly adapt to. However, what does appear to cause behavioural problems is the partial loss of sight in one eye. Indeed, it has often been said that one eye is of more use to a horse than one-and-a-half.

Question
I have had my Thoroughbred mare, Roxette, for six months now and she continues to be terrible in traffic. Heavy lorries are her worst fear, especially if they are coming towards her. She usually bounces up and down and threatens to bolt back to the stables. Cows are her other great fear, so you can imagine what a nightmare she is to ride on country roads: cattle can send her shooting away from the hedge into the path of her other bogeymen, the juggernauts. I hack in company most days, but she does not seem to improve. In fact, since the onset of winter, I think she's actually getting worse. Why should this be so? More to the point, what can you suggest to sort her out?

Answer

You don't say how your mare is managed but, as winter approaches, most people start to increase concentrate rations and bring their horses in at night. Both of these factors are likely to increase Roxette's reactivity.

Concentrates lead to greater excitability, and so each lorry precipitates an exaggerated response. The other reason that winter may be associated with a deterioration in her tolerance of heavy traffic could be to do with the increase in rainfall compared with the summer months. In my experience, horses that are frightened of traffic are far more reactive when the roads are wet because the traffic noise is dramatically amplified. Although every winter day is not wetter than every summer day, the prevalence of surface water on roads during the winter months means that this is when the fear of traffic is least likely to be extinguished.

Classically, there are two ways of overcoming fear in horses: habituation and counter-conditioning. Both techniques aim to teach new responses to fear-eliciting stimuli – in this case, cows and lorries. I advise you to approach these two issues separately so that your mare gets over her fear of cattle before you start exposing her to traffic again. Some horses are very dangerous in heavy traffic, and Roxette clearly falls into this category when she is leaping into the road in a bid to avoid cows on the other side of the hedgerow.

In counter-conditioning the aim is to teach the horse to expect something pleasant to accompany the fear-eliciting stimulus. This is useful with fear of being handled, for instance, but does not work so well where the source of the fear is a third party such as a cow. The tendency is for horses to associate being calm in the presence of the stimulus as dependent on the presence of the trainer.

The approach I recommend for your mare is habituation. With this technique, as the name suggests, the aim is to get her used to being exposed to the fear-eliciting stimulus. First of all, you need to be absolutely certain what it is about cows that upsets Roxette so much. For instance, it may be that the colour of certain breeds has unpleasant associations. If this is the case, you will have to select cows of those breeds to use in your therapy. You will also need to win the co-operation of a local farmer. Youngstock are perhaps the

Some horses are very dangerous in heavy traffic.

worst animals to choose for such an exercise because they are incorrigibly nosy and, having begun to investigate, they tend to charge around and spook the horse still further. The best strategy to adopt is to put Roxette in a small paddock with a single mature cow as her only field-mate. She will soon learn that her fears are unfounded and that she can even relate to the cow as a companion.

A similar approach can then be used for her fear of traffic. Grazing beside the road in a small paddock with sound fencing is the only way to expose a horse to a continual flow of vehicles. Naturally, most traffic-shy animals will graze those parts of the field that are farthest from the road, but if they are left in the paddock for long enough, feeding closer and closer to the highway becomes the only means of meeting nutritional requirements. In this way a horse will gradually habituate itself to the sight, smell and sound of heavy traffic.

Once Roxette is feeding happily beside the road, the next stage is to hand-graze her on verges and give any bucket-feeds on the roadside. Use a bridle to maximise your control of her; you really need as much control as possible, and you cannot afford to worry that she may find chewing difficult with a bit in her mouth. An additional safety tip: wear gloves and carry a schooling-whip to avoid being bounced on by an alarmed horse. Do not feed her titbits, because the temptation will be to give them in association with the unwanted behaviour as a way of calming her. This could teach your horse that jumping is a sure means of getting you to surrender your goodies. A full meal in a container on the ground is far better because she will learn that taking her head out of the bucket to clown around means the absence of something pleasant.

Since the aim is to change Roxette's behaviour when ridden you should tack her up for these training sessions to prevent her from learning that traffic is only innocuous when riding is not involved. The next step is to ask a friend to hold her while you sit on her back. This process takes months rather than weeks, but is worth doing properly because, as I'm sure you realise, horses can be very dangerous in traffic. In the UK they are involved in an average of eight traffic-related accidents a day, so it is simply not worth taking any chances.

Sleeping

Question
Shannon, my Highland pony gelding, never seems to lie down, even on the thickest fresh bedding. I am slightly concerned that he has something wrong with his hindlegs or his back that means he is worried about being unable to get back up again once he is on the ground. Can you explain why he doesn't ever seem to want to take the weight off his feet?

Answer
The most succinct answer to this inquiry is probably: Because he doesn't really need to! The survival advantage

that sleeping upright brought to horses as they evolved means that it is a behaviour that was selected for – horses that were dependent on lying down as a means of getting some rest and relaxation were more likely to be selected as sitting targets by predators. For some herbivores, lying on the ground is acceptable because this is how they can most readily ruminate. Unlike ruminants, horses digest their food in the hind-gut and so do not have to rely on this form of regurgitation as a way of breaking food down.

I would not worry that Shannon is not getting enough sleep, because there are structures in his legs that take the strain and carry his weight without him having to concentrate on contracting muscles or keeping upright. These supporting structures allow horses to stand without becoming tired. Fears about getting up are not the reason for your pony's resolve to remain standing, because horses do not seem to worry about future events. I can say this with some confidence because the horses that have the greatest trouble rising are the ones that get cast (trapped against the side of the box while trying to get to their feet). And these poor characters get cast time and time again because they never learn to avoid lying in boxes that are too small for them to get up in.

If the bedding you are offering Shannon is good and thick, I would not worry about the choice he makes to remain on his feet. Indeed, horses that start to spend large chunks of their day on the ground are a far greater cause for concern because they may be experiencing foot pain such as that caused by laminitis.

Snaking

Stallions in a free-ranging environment are often spotted swinging their heads from side to side, with both head and neck extended. Records of this behaviour in feral horse populations show that it is mainly used by a stallion to move his harem away from other males or other groups. It is also an effective method of grouping the harem, since mares tend to congregate as soon as they notice the display. However, since it can reliably elicit movement in general, the characteristic action is also occasionally used to drive individuals away – for example, to banish colts from the harem.

Snaking is often misinterpreted by human observers as

bullying or even as a form of dominance. In fact, rank has very little to do with the way in which horses respond to this signal. Sometimes mares respond not just by moving but also by urinating while on the move. It could be that they are giving off scent in order to confirm that they are part of the stallion's harem. It has also been speculated that it is a way of pacifying him, but this would imply anger on his part. This is rather an anthropomorphic interpretation: stallions may *seem* annoyed to the human observer, but we cannot be sure what emotions they experience.

Just as some bitches cock their legs, mares occasionally show forms of masculine behaviour. By adopting the snaking strategy, for example, some mares have been known to guard other members of their groups from the advances of strange horses.

Snapping
Commonest in the second month of a foal's life, when he is making the bravest of sorties from his mother's side in order to approach other horses, snapping is a signal of submission. In the same way that pups race up to adult dogs and throw themselves on their backs in submission, foals need to socialise with other members of the herd and in order to do so safely they snap their mouths as they approach as a way of minimising any aggression. It may seem strange that this mouthing action is not misinterpreted as an attempt to bite, but it is often accompanied by a characteristic lip-smacking noise and is not associated with any other aggressive cues such as pinned-back ears. In addition, the head is raised as part of the behaviour, thus distinguishing it from the more menacing snaking approach of a horse who really means to pick a fight.

Foals snap primarily at elders, but will occasionally snap at other foals. There is no difference between colts and fillies in the rate of snapping and both sexes have been recorded snapping occasionally until their third year of life. It is an extremely rare behaviour in adults. The important thing to remember is that it is basically a response to horse shapes of a certain size. They do occasionally get it wrong, and this is why foals can be seen snapping at cows, which haven't the slightest notion of how to respond to such a bizarre display.

Young mares during their first oestrus period will often show this response, in combination with other fear displays, when they receive novel invitations and advances from stallions.

Question
I have an Arab mare with a four-month-old foal at foot. Yesterday for the first time since she foaled, I rode her, in the paddock. The colt followed behind for a while and then got really stroppy, throwing his head around and trying to bite me. He is usually very placid, so you can understand how disturbing it was for me to have to beat a hasty retreat from a foal of this age. Do you think early castration would stop him being aggressive?

Answer
I think your colt failed to recognise the combination of you and his mum. What you have described is a perfectly normal response for a foal that had simply encountered a new large animal. The mouthing action is not an attempt to bite but an attempt to appease, and has developed as a part of young horse behaviour that allows exploration without provoking hostility from other horses. If your foal is the only youngster in the field he probably craves the opportunity to play, and this would account for his head-tossing display. Since he has merely been playing with and submitting to you, castration is not called for at this stage.

Essentially, the decision about when it is best to castrate is a matter of individual owner choice, and is often prompted when a colt has become too much of a handful. While I prefer to see colts that have been allowed to grow a mature crest, I realise that some owners have neither the time nor the inclination to wrestle with adolescent exuberance. Furthermore, I feel that when they are intimidated by coltish behaviour they are best advised to seek early castration, since so much aggression can be learned at this stage in a horse's life. Owners often inadvertently teach their young horses to throw their weight around by backing off from them when they are experimenting with displays of aggression.

Social facilitation

If you observe a paddock of horses for an hour or two, you will notice that if one starts to graze, others in the group soon follow suit. This phenomenon, which describes the influence that one animal can have on its associates, is called *social facilitation*. It is especially common among herd animals, and seems to involve subconscious brain processes. Take as a further example the swerving of a group of horses, first to the left and then to the right, when fleeing a potential predator. These changes in direction do not occur because every one of the group has seen the various manoeuvres of the predator, but because those that *can* see have the ability to influence the movement of the rest. The initiator of an activity, or 'social facilitator', is not selected by rank.

Drinking is another behaviour pattern that is often initiated by social facilitation. In this instance, though, once the group arrives at the water source, rank does play a part, with the dominant members of the herd being the first to drink even though the whole herd has moved to the water source together under the initiation of an individual. On the other hand, when horses roll – another behaviour that occurs in sequence throughout a group as a result of social facilitation – rank plays no part whatsoever.

T

Tail-chewing

Question
I have recently weaned a home-bred Irish Draught foal, whom I call Jake, from his mum and put him in a paddock with a retired point-to-pointer. They spend all day together and never seem to fight over the concentrates and hay that I give them. But yesterday morning I went to the field to check them, and found my poor old horse walking around with almost no tail. He looked like one of those docked horses in an old hunting painting. There is plenty to eat on the pasture that these horses share, so why did my foal suddenly decide to mutilate his friend in this way and what should I do?

Answer
Play is one explanation, since foals are often seen with rather strange toys in their mouths and have even been reported to throw sticks which they subsequently appear to retrieve like an enthusiastic Labrador puppy. The animation that a tail shows when attached to a companion may be sufficient to lure a foal with an inquisitive mouth. The subsequent chewing and ingestion of the tail hairs are less easy to explain. Colts are in my experience the keenest of all horses to use their mouths to entertain themselves in this way, and the fact that your own youngster has no peer company – no field-mates of the same age – points to this as the most obvious cause.

Taste deterrents sometimes work as a short-term cure, but they do not address any underlying need.

I'm afraid the most obvious cure is to provide Jake with appropriate company. You do not have to buy another youngster, because more and more part-time breeders find themselves in your position every year. They would like to wean their youngstock as naturally as possible but usually end up turning them out with an unplayful old-timer or, worse still, with no equine company at all. The more I learn about horses, the more I am convinced of their need for appropriate company. I suggest that you advertise locally for a foal in the same predicament, preferably of the same sex, and bring the two together. Both foals will benefit, as will both owners, because foals kept at pasture in this way are always easier to handle in the long run.

Some experts have shown that horses on low-fibre diets are the most likely to take up this habit, and have concluded that it is a possible way of meeting the needs that each horse has for fibre. Although it is difficult to completely refute this explanation, I feel that it is unlikely to be the whole story, since manes are less readily consumed and more suitable fibre sources such as tree bark are often ignored in favour of tail hair.

Malice should be ruled out since, contrary to the opinions of some owners, this is not an emotion that can be readily applied to non-human animals, especially the social variety.

You do not mention the presence of any other occupants in the field apart from the two horses, but other stock such as calves are often responsible for the overnight disappearance of horse tails. Another possibility is that accumulations of micronutrients such as trace elements are more attractive than the tail itself. For instance, it has been suggested that a dirty tail can be attractive to nosy neighbours because it can hold aggregations of sweat which can prove irresistibily salty. The attention paid to salt-licks from time to time indicates that when horses are short of sodium chloride and find a source of this mineral they tend to capitalise on it. So this may be behind some episodes of tail-chewing.

Teeth

Question
Every year I ask my vet to check our old Shetland mare's teeth when he comes to give her a vaccination booster. It's really comical watching the poor chap kneeling in the straw in front of the little pony, as he backs her into a corner

and puts the rasp in her mouth. She always looks terribly apprehensive, with her eyes rolling round in her head, but she never seems to mind when he actually starts rasping. I'm sure she would tell us if something was amiss – she certainly puts him in his place if he tries to do anything that she does not approve of. But why does she tolerate this procedure? It seems quite bizarre to me, but not to her! More to the point, why do some horses have to be sedated for this routine job?

Answer

There have certainly been instances of horses steadily grinding their own molars against one another when sharp spurs and cusps develop, so we should not be so surprised that this behaviour is tolerated when we do it for them. All the same, the fact that they put up with the noise and sensation of having this job done for them by a stranger for up to twenty minutes *is* often surprising.

The teeth of most grazing animals are designed to grow throughout life as a means of replacing the grinding surface which is in use for almost every waking hour. For this reason, there are no nerve endings at the surface of their molar teeth. When vets use rasps to remove sharp spurs that have made chewing or ridden work uncomfortable, they are really only targeting irregularities at the surface of the teeth. So the extent to which the patient can feel this abrasive process is minimal.

Occasionally, when one spot has to be concentrated on, friction can heat up the mouth and this may cause some horses to back off. In novices this is due to generalised fear, and they should be approached with tremendous tact in the same way that foot-shy youngsters should be dealt with. Some animals remain generally difficult to handle around the mouth, and it is memories of clumsy and insensitive rasping episodes that are the main source of fear in older horses.

Pain during tooth-rasping can arise if the horse moves, or if the vet is unfortunate enough to slip and send the rasp into the side of the cheek or inadvertently finds himself rasping the tongue instead of the teeth! Such mishaps can put a horse off rasping for life. One is reminded of the Jack Russell terrier who puts up with having his toe-nails clipped until one day the vet nips the quick of his claws by mistake.

(As many vets will testify, this marks the cessation of co-operation on the dog's part.) It seems, therefore, that the first experiences of unusual veterinary procedures are extremely formative of patient's future attitude to them. It is likely that the first time anyone ever rasped your mare's teeth she or he took a great deal of time and patience over the job. This will have helped to ensure that the pony stood still and was less likely to interfere with the careful and pain-free execution of the procedure.

Territory

As we discussed earlier, social behaviour in feral horse populations is more common than territorial behaviour, in that if one band of horses encounters another, any defensiveness shown usually appears to be an attempt to maintain the integrity of the band rather than to defend the site. Exceptions to this rule have been recorded on narrow barrier islands such as Shackleford Island in the United States, where two-thirds of harem groups maintain well defended permanent territories which do not overlap. Under free-range conditions, even where the territory is extensive, group bonding is important to the extent that horses maintain visual contact with each other continually.

Stud piles are often arranged along the fence line by domestic stallions because this is the area closest to the ranges of other animals.

Tipping

Question

I have an Anglo-Arab gelding called Zebedee who has been with the family for most of his life. He is a great character on the yard and is always the first to call out when anyone comes out of the house. He does a reasonable amount of work during the summer but things calm down in the winter after the showing season ends. I tend to keep him in (during the winter) because he hates the cold and just stands shivering in a corner of the field if I leave him out.

My inquiry revolves around his feeding behaviour, which leaves a lot to be desired. You see, Zebedee gets really worked up when it's time for his evening meal. As soon as it arrives he starts bobbing his head around and threatening me, which doesn't matter because I know that he would never hurt me. Once I have put the feed tub on the ground, his interest naturally darts away from me and towards the tub. You'd think that he would want to concentrate on eating, but instead he starts by tipping the tub and sending the food all over the floor. He spends ages picking it out of his bedding but, of course, he loses some of his ration with this foolish trick. I have every intention of putting a bracket on the wall to hold the tub securely off the ground, or at least asking my husband to do so. In the meantime, can you explain why Zebedee wastes his food in this way?

Answer
You will have noticed that Zebedee's apparent inadequacy is almost exclusively linked to food buckets rather than to water buckets, so it's safe to assume that it has more to do with the contents of the bucket than being unable to use the bucket itself. There is no equivalent in feral horse behaviour for eating concentrate food out of a bucket. The nearest useful parallel might be when a horse at grass finds a particularly succulent and tasty patch of grasses at the peak of their bloom. Knowing that other horses may be observing him for any clues that he has won the day's lottery, he does what he must to get food into his mouth as swiftly as possible. Savouring one's food is not a wise move in such a scenario.

The flavours of concentrates in the bucket of our stabled horse are made all the more real by his mouthing them and going through all the time-honoured muzzle movements that have been involved in the prehension of food since the invention of the hoof. In the same way as a child chews gum with overstated relish and may end up chewing her own cheek, the overmotivated horse performs all of the behaviours associated with a good meal but, in doing so, spills it and makes it less easy to eat and probably less tasty.

The other problem that many owners report is that the horse doesn't just tip the food over – he then picks up the feed tub in his teeth and throws it around the box. Zebedee may well go on to develop this trick unless you fasten the bucket to the wall. Additionally, it usually helps to place a large smooth stone in the bottom of the bucket so that the horse has to actively forage around and even underneath the obstacle to obtain his ration. This extra work will absorb some of the overexcitement that Zebedee associates with meal-times.

Twitch

Question
My vet tends to use a twitch whenever he does rectal examinations on my old brood mare. She is a fairly easygoing character generally, but she does get rather touchy about her rear end. I can understand his reasons for wanting to protect himself, but I still have reservations about him routinely using the twitch. The mare gets very stroppy when she knows that she is going to be twitched. Can you explain how it works and whether it is humane?

Answer
Whether it takes the form of twisting rope or a hinged pair of smooth metal rods, the twitch works by applying pressure to the nerve endings in the sensitive tip of the upper lip. In other words, it works by causing pain. This is thought to release endorphins, the body's own pain-killing chemicals in the brain. It is difficult to say whether using the twitch is humane, because very little research has been done on the subject. By 'getting stroppy' your mare is making it plain that she can remember the tightening of the twitch as unpleasant. The puzzle is that, while some horses make it quite clear that they would rather not be twitched, others do not seem to object. The alternative in many cases is intravenous sedation, which also involves an initial burst of pain. Since we know that some horses resent injections more than being twitched, it would seem that each case should be considered on its own merits. In either case, it is important to be certain that there is a real need for extra control rather than simply adopting strong-arm tactics from the word go.

The fact that the soporific effect of endorphins released in the brain in this way does not seem to last more then twenty minutes means that for protracted procedures, including clipping, it is best to call a break after approximately fifteen minutes to allow the endorphin-producing sites in the brain to become refreshed. As a rule of thumb, the tension on a twitch should be just sufficient to stop the upper lip wriggling. Any tightness beyond this limit can cause damage to the lip by occluding its blood supply. Rope-loop twitches should not be of man-made fibres or of twines that can damage the skin. In my opinion, twitching the ears or the tongue is unjustifiable, not least because of the risk of damage to these more sensitive structures.

Finally, from the point of view of human safety, it is imperative that you bear in mind that a horse is capable of rearing, striking and even cow-kicking in response to being twitched.

U

Urinating

Question
I realise that it is not exactly a burning issue, but could you explain why my horse stales every time I put him in his stable after a ride? The tedious thing is that he always does it on fresh bedding, which is rather wasteful. My husband says that it's all a conspiracy to make horse-keeping as expensive as possible! I know that my horse does not see things this way, but why does he make a mess of his clean, dry bed as soon as possible? Wouldn't he prefer to have a clean bed, for a short while at least?

Answer
I suspect that your routine involves you taking your horse out of his box, mucking him out, bedding him down, riding him and then putting him back in his box. If he is doing mainly road work, the combination of this routine and his workload means that he has to go for some time without standing on a surface that is favourable for urination. When he finally gets back on to a suitable surface – the bedding in his box – it is not the freshness of the bedding material that makes him content to empty his bladder so much as the relief of being on a surface that is less likely to cause splash-back. The smells of urine and faeces are also likely to be concentrated in his box, and it is believed that these encourage him to urinate, just as wild horses often add to midden piles.

The Jockey Club have put these behavioural quirks to good use in their search for 'banned substances' in race-horses. Many of the drugs that affect performance are passed in urine, so Jockey Club stewards, under the direction of veterinary surgeons, are often keen to obtain urine samples from horses once they have finished a race. To do this, they place the horse in a box with used bedding – a reliable stimulus for urination in almost all horses. Occasionally, potty-proud individuals need to have blood or saliva samples taken but the vast majority provide ample urine as soon they walk into the box. Being made to stand on concrete before being tested is a recognised method of ensuring that there is urine in the bladder when the staff attempt to collect it. (This is why owners who push their horses' bedding to the sides of the box during the day find that their horses urinate in the evening after their beds are replaced.)

Used bedding is more effective than fresh because the scent of other horses prompts marking behaviour. Because urination occurs when the horse is brought into the box, some observers mistakenly regard this phenomenon as a kind of territorial behaviour. Horses do not have territories in the same way that cats and dogs do. If they did, then the first thing that they would do in a new paddock would be to mark it with urine or faeces.

In well drained loose-boxes with sufficient litter, the ritual sprinklings that some horses offer when they enter their boxes are of little consequence to straw and shavings bills. However, if marital harmony dictates that you are seen to economise there are recognised ways of targeting urine away from the bedding. Ultimately, the best way to avoid bed-wetting for short periods is to keep your horse's bladder less full by giving him as many opportunities as possible to urinate before he is put in his box. Getting off his back is an ideal way of signalling to him that his contact with concrete and tarmac is over for the day. You should also be able to hand-graze him in a spot that you know has previously been marked with urine and wait there with him until he stales. If he already responds to auditory cues such as whistling or straw-shaking, then so much the better if these can be used to encourage the behaviour that you want. Gently scratching his neck when he does urinate is sufficient as a reinforcer to help confirm to him that he is doing the right thing. This system of timing, positioning and prompting works to build up new associations in your horse's brain and will be rapidly adopted as his routine as long as you are consistent.

V

Vocalisation

Depending on one's definition, it is possible to recognise four types of noise that a normal horse produces from its larynx: squeals, nickers, whinnies and groans. Other familiar noises that do not involve the larynx include snorts, blows and snores. The study of these vocalisations has required the development of spectographic devices that plot the sounds on a graph and explain the differences between them.

Squeals are usually associated with aggressive or threatening encounters such as can occur between a mare and a courting stallion. Given that these sounds are used to warn off unwelcome attention, it is strange that they are so rarely used in anticipation of the pain of being treated by a veterinarian or of being ridden by a particularly unforgiving rider. Could it be that horses know that such vocal signals can only be understood by members of their own species?

Nickers are emitted by horses in anticipation of food, by stallions in anticipation of sex and by mares when they display concern for their foals. In the absence of their mothers, foals often follow humans more readily if they hear them mimicking this sort of nicker. The same noise is found as a food-related greeting signal in some horses and is used by some owners to invite their horses to come and be caught in the paddock.

Often beginning with a squeal and ending with a nicker, whinnies or neighs are the noises most often used for relocating an affiliate. This is because these sounds are highly differentiated between individuals, and for this reason they are also heard in response to the departure of a herd member and, in an attempt to rally the group, upon arrival at a new yard or paddock. Foals are capable of responding to their dam's whinny rather than that of another mare from approximately two weeks of age. This ties in neatly with the onset of their maturing courage and desire to explore.

Groans are most often associated with stabled horses in states of low arousal – for example, a horse being starved for twelve hours before surgery or an animal in prolonged discomfort such as a foaling mare struggling to deliver a badly presented foetus. Another predictable instance of groaning is when horses rise from a snooze on the ground, and certainly when they swim. The latter circumstance seems to alter both laryngeal position and lung function, which is why each exhalation in a swimming horse can bring with it unusual stimulation of the vocal cords.

Among the non-laryngeal noises the snort and the blow are perhaps the most familiar. Snorting is heard when a horse clears his airways of dust, but it can also result from frustration – for example, when a dam loses her foal during traditional weaning. And when a horse encounters an interesting odour, blowing occurs as an expiratory flushing of the airways after a bout of sniffing.

Vomeronasal organ

Also known as Jacobson's organ, the vomeronasal organ is a specialised smelling device found in many mammals. In horses it is housed in the roof of the mouth, and has two lobes that extend for approximately 12 cm (5 ins) as blind-ending tubes from just behind the upper incisor teeth towards the brain. These tubes are lined with nerve endings that send information about pheromones on a hot-line straight to the olfactory cortex of the brain. Unlike the dog and cat, the horse has a vomeronasal organ that does not communicate with the mouth, and so its activation does not rely on licking behaviour.

This organ is especially suited for sampling chemicals of low volatility from other animals and is assisted by gravity and by the nose wrinkling that is seen when a horse shows flehmen (see p. 138). These pheromones, which are detected in excreta and remain stable for weeks, serve as a record of the excreting animal's sex hormone level.

The vomeronasal organ is exquisitely sensitive and can help to inflame the passion of a red-blooded male several miles from a mare in season. In a bid to make colts and stallions easier to handle in public – at race meetings, for instance – handlers often smear their horses' nostrils with menthol or eucalyptus preparations, which can mask the incoming smell of mares. But great care should be taken to avoid contact with the sensitive lining of the nasal cavity when applying these rather irritating materials.

W

Water

Question
I have a show Arab called Mistakett who excels in county-level competition and seems quite promising as a racing prospect. He is a great exhibitionist and gets very excited when I begin to get him ready for a show. When it comes to shampooing him, however, excitement turns into outright drama with hind legs kicking out and front legs stamping with temper. Things go from bad to worse when I start to rinse him off. He never seems to be able to cope with this procedure, and I am hoping that you may be able to tell me why this is so.

Answer
Feral horses may seek shelter under trees and beside bushes in driving rain, but their needs for nutrition often outweigh any desire to keep dry. Grazing in the rain is made tolerable by strategic orientation of the body so that the horse's hindquarters are pointed upwind to take the brunt of the precipitation. The direction of hair growth all over the body is also useful as a means of channelling off the water. Places such as under the tail-head, the udder and the sheath, inside the ears and under the eyes, all tend to remain relatively dry in even the most torrential downpours.

Some horses relish the sensation of a jet of water on certain parts of their bodies while resenting it in others. Jets of tap-driven water into areas of the body that are designed to remain snug, dry and as crusty as possible are aversive to many horses. Getting these parts wet is not only unfamiliar to most horses, it is also hellishly ticklish. Many fidget in an attempt to avoid the tickle rather than the moisture itself,

Some horses are more ticklish than others.

and Mistakett appears to be one of these. The shampooing phase of his regular baths is the cue that a severe tickling is about to follow and this is why he begins to wriggle at this point. But it is the rinsing that follows which sends rivulets of cooling water scurrying across his face and down his thighs in the most unpredictable and unbearable fashion. On the whole, most animals prefer warm water from a bucket rather than cold from a tap, so bear this in mind whenever you wash Mistakett. Ultimately, however, just like humans some horses are more ticklish than others. With a warm-blooded, thin-skinned animal like an Arab, there is very little you can do to overcome it because it is a reflex behaviour initiated by unpredictable stimuli.

But there is another possible approach to your problem. It is being recognised that thorough grooming is the best way to get fresh sebum from the skin onto the hair shafts of an animal's coat – sebum is the greasy natural conditioner that gives coats their shine and works to help shed dirt from the hair shafts. Regular shampooing is thought to effectively remove more sebum than it generates, thereby making the coat less resistant to grime and generating the need for more and more baths. Assuming that Mistakett can cope with being enthusiastically groomed, this may be the best way to accommodate both his need for fewer baths and your need for a shiny show specimen.

Question
I keep my New Forest pony, Becky, on a small private yard close to home but I only get to see her in the evenings. This is because the yard manager routinely turns all the horses out in the morning, leaving it to me to bring her in at night. Unfortunately, this system has been altered recently because we have had so much rain. In fact, the weather has been so bad that we have been asked to keep our horses off the fields altogether in order to avoid them getting poached. We all agreed to this but now I'm beginning to regret it because I'm sure my horse is becoming bored. For the last three evenings I have found her playing with the automatic watering bowl. Her bed has been soaking wet and quite dug up. What should I do?

Answer
While playing with water buckets and dribbling their contents back out of the mouth via a rather self-satisfied droopy lower lip is a fairly common part of normal horse behaviour, it can become an obsession in some individuals. It is also known that horses suffering from a blockage in their gullet ('choke') and those with early grass disease may stand over their water for hours on end in a characteristically doleful fashion. The wetness of the bed could be the consequence of overflow from the bowl or of the passage of unusually large volumes of urine.

As a first step, spend time with Becky to check that she is not experiencing any swallowing problems. I'd also like you to check that she is not spending excessive time with the salt-lick – I have known this to cause dramatic surges in water demand. It is vital to define the problem you are dealing with, and your vet will certainly appreciate as much information as you can offer about the situation before he starts taking blood samples in his quest for a diagnosis.

The next step is to weigh your mare at a public weigh-bridge or livestock market. Then, block off the water supply to the automatic bowl, and replace this water source with buckets positioned on large plastic trays to catch most of the drips. This way you can work out how much your mare is actually consuming and how much she is dribbling out of her mouth. With these two pieces of data you can calculate Becky's water-consumption in litres per kilogram (quarts per pound). This figure should be useful to your vet as an indication of the current severity of her condition, and also as a bench-mark against which to measure any improvement or deterioration associated with treatment.

Armed with all the facts, your vet will be better able to decide what laboratory tests he would like to perform that might explain Becky's increased water intake. If he rules out any physiological reason, the diagnosis will point towards a behavioural problem. Water intake can become excessive as a result of stereotypic drinking and/or salt-licking in response to an inadequate environment. The history of her increased demand for water arising at the same time as her move from the fields into the stable supports a behavioural diagnosis. If treatment is instituted promptly, resolution of her behaviour is thankfully more likely than for other stereotypies. The treatment does not involve limiting the supply of salt or water, but instead relies on redirecting her attention to more appropriate behaviour.

Faced with this diagnosis, it is really up to you to improve Becky's environmental conditions and increase the time that she spends out of her stable. My own research has shown that the more time a horse spends out of his box, the less likely he is to become frustrated by the absence of a free-range lifestyle.

Unfortunately, many owners feel that maximising time out of the stable is not an option in the winter. Naturally, I would agree that the winter is a challenging time for many horsekeepers, what with the hazards of dark nights which limit the amount of exercise that can be given and the constant threat of mud fever, which restricts access to boggy paddocks, especially for horses with white legs.

However, there are ways of coping with the factors that limit a horse's time out of the stable. For instance, in the case of traffic-proof horses, relying on the fact that equine night-vision is better than human one can overcome the lack of light by exercising with stirrup lights and fluorescent strips. Mud fever is a thornier problem, but experience seems to point to the early use of barrier cream on clipped lower limbs as a fruitful means of prevention. If there is an all-weather surface available, horses should be allowed to socialise whenever it is not being used for ridden work. As the winter advances, storage barns begin to empty and so these too can be used as small common-rooms for affiliated horses. By normalising horse behaviour patterns, the use of diverse environments in this way can bring tremendous dividends.

The idea behind all of these strategies is to introduce a new equilibrium into Becky's day, so that she can see her stable as a place for eating and resting, not drinking. By maximising her workload you will minimise the amount of time she spends idling in her box. Additionally, you will increase her demands for food and thereby promote her motivation to forage, which can be met by the ad lib provision of hay in fine-holed hay nets.

Weaving

Weaving is the name given to the side-to-side rocking of the head, shoulders and sometimes even the whole body that some horses perform as a stereotypy. Formerly described as a stable vice, weaving is believed by some owners to cause wear and tear to the hooves. It is not clear whether this is actually the case – indeed, some racehorse trainers believe that it helps to fend off tendon injuries. What is of more concern is the likelihood that weaving signals that the weaver is either currently suffering or underwent some sort of mental discomfort when the behaviour first developed.

My own research has revealed that approximately one in every twenty Thoroughbreds is a weaver. To some this figure seems surprisingly high, but one has to bear in mind that not all horses weave with equal enthusiasm. While most weavers will develop the behaviour when they are stabled and perform it only at times of excitement, rare individuals start at the age of one month and continue to weave, even in the field. The animals with the most dramatic case histories are often members of families that are known to be predisposed to this behavioural abnormality.

Peaks in weaving over a twenty-four-hour period tend to coincide with periods of anticipation and heightened arousal. For instance, in a hungry horse bouts of weaving may be initiated by a number of stimuli, such as the clatter of buckets, the sight of an owner arriving and the greeting

Weaving can cause wear-and-tear to the hooves.

sounds of other horses, all of which confirm that supper-time has arrived once more. Weaving also peaks when horses move about on the yard, whether arriving or departing. This happens because, being such social animals, they find thwarted following responses very frustrating to deal with. Similarly, even when turned out, weavers can be seen weaving at the gate if they can see affiliated horses being taken away from them or if they feel it is time they were brought in.

Weaving is thought to be linked to the locomotory system in the same way that crib-biting is thought to be linked to the digestive system. I would have to say that I agree with this since the weaving horse is showing that he wants to get going and any barrier will be the source of considerable frustration. Weaving has not been shown to be associated with the release of endorphins, as is the case with crib-biting, so at the moment pharmaceutical approaches to this behavioural quirk are not foreseen.

Controversy surrounds stereotypies, and while preventing them from occurring is, given all the uncertainties that remain, the only humane option, we have to bear in mind that preventing the expression of established behaviours, which could in fact be coping mechanisms, may serve to reduce an animal's welfare.

Question

I have owned Blue, a Highland mare, for three weeks. She was purchased from a local abattoir for the price of her carcass. She was very distressed when I led her away from her companion, continually calling to him, and she started to defaecate profusely as she left the yard. I put her into a loose-box and she immediately started weaving over the stable door. She had continued to do this, with the typical lateral swaying of her head, neck and forequarters whenever she knows that I'm getting her food ready or when she sees another horse come or go. Sometimes she even lifts her forelimbs in time with each oscillation, and occasionally also her hindlimbs. This is accompanied by repeated neighing and intermittent box-walking.

I erected an anti-weaving cradle, but this meant that when Blue did any weaving she had to do it within the confines of the loose-box itself rather than over the stable door. This effectively reduced the size of the stable that she has to use and so I have dispensed with the cradle. Friends of mine who keep their horses on my yard are concerned that the behaviour will spread. Is this true? What, if anything, can I do to help her, and can you explain why she weaves at these specific times?

Answer

Although we have tremendous difficulty in proving that horses are capable of learning even the most basic information by observation, some owners are convinced that weaving is transmissible by mimicry. Much more research needs to be done in this area before we can be sure that a normal horse can copy a stereotypic behaviour. The usual story is that a horse arrives on a yard, is stabled next-door to a weaver and soon starts weaving. The thorny problem here is that we cannot be certain that it is not the general management rather than the equine neighbour's demonstration that has prompted the behaviour in the new arrival. Furthermore, it is even possible that the presence of a weaving neighbour may simply make being in a stable more aversive than it would otherwise be for a normal horse. In this case, weaving may simply be the hitherto normal horse's way of coping with this sort of unwelcome environmental factor. Either way, once weaving has started, the chances are that it will continue regardless of attempts at prevention (*see also* Crib-biting, p. 111).

As with stereotypies in other species, weaving in horses can become dissociated from its precipitating causes as the animals age. Treatment of these behaviours is rarely complete, which may be because they can become self-rewarding if the brain releases endorphins. Furthermore, one must bear in mind that aversion to being housed in a stable may differ between breeds of horses, so that ameliorating adverse management factors may also have a limited effectiveness. For example, if a critical period of daily confinement is necessary for the development of stereotypic behaviour, this critical period may be shorter in horses that are genetically predisposed to weaving. It is also possible that all horses find the stable environment aversive and that sterotypies represent a coping response of which only certain horses are capable. The extent to which a confirmed weaver can be encouraged to perform normal rather then stereotyped behaviour in the stable would seem to depend on how successful the owner is in making the stable less aversive. Therefore, becoming able to manage and control the frequency and intensity are more likely than a complete cure.

Your experience with the anti-weaving cradle is not unusual. Sometimes, it seems, putting an obstacle at the stable door is not only ineffectual but also serves to thwart the occupant's need to express its frustration with its current environment. The anecdotal link between the sight of a stable companion departing and the onset of a bout of weaving is a common one, which only goes to underline the fact that your mare finds social isolation particularly aversive. Fitting her stable with bars and grilles to replace the blank wall, so that she can see and touch her neighbours, will reduce her frustration level. And although it may sound uncomfortably radical, you should also consider replacing the front of her box with a gate, so as to improve her visual access to the comings and goings on the yard. This will increase her level of general stimulation and thereby reduce her tendency to oscillate from extreme arousal to 'boredom'.

Horses respond to stylised two-dimensional images of horses, reacting in times of heightened stress as they would to an affiliated member of the same species (or conspecific). I am currently investigating the use of safety-backed mirrors (2 × 2 metres or 6 × 6 feet) in the stables of weavers. The results of experiments with four horses have all been promising, with the animals appearing to move towards the mirrors at times of peak frustration and standing quietly beside their reflections rather than weaving at the stable door. So I would also advocate the introduction of a mirror, as a way of enriching your mare's environment. The only snag with this visual display is that, occasionally, horses glare and pull unpleasant faces at their reflections while eating their hay. If this happens try not to let Blue catch you laughing at her, and discreetly move the mirror and the hay net as far as possible apart from one another!

Whiskers
Whiskers on the muzzle are an important part of the equipment with which a horse senses its environment. The base of each of these *vibrissae* had a pocket of blood vessels around it which amplifies any movement of the hair itself, so that it can be easily detected by the nerve cells that send messages to the brain about hair movement. One of the most important reasons for this apparatus in the horse is that, given that it has evolved to spend so long with its head to the ground and its eyes on the surroundings, the ability to feel around with a network of hairs means that its attention can simultaneously be paid to the possible approach of predators. As evolution has had its way with the horse's visual field, the ground directly below its grazing nose being

effectively a blind spot, whiskers have become even more important.

The common practice of clipping the whiskers of a horse's muzzle for purely cosmetic reasons is therefore a very selfish move on the part of owners, since clipping impairs its ability to sense the proximity and contours of the land it grazes and to feel its way around its stable. An equivalent imposition for humans would be to make them eat all their meals wearing a pair of mittens and a balaclava. Admittedly, adaptation would eventually occur, but not before a long period of considerable frustration.

Wood-chewing
Wood-chewing most often occurs when the stabled horse runs out of hay, but horses in paddocks chew wood, too, and the behaviour has also been reported in feral horses, so it is quite unhelpful to persist in calling it a 'stable vice'. Because it is recorded in free-ranging animals, wood-chewing is regarded by many behavioural scientists as a normal feature of horse behaviour. Indeed, there are some owners who actively encourage their horses to chew wood by giving them logs to munch. The vast majority of owners, though, do not go along with this.

In my own surveys, I found that wood-chewing was the most unwelcome of all abnormal behaviours – because of the expense of the damage caused by the habit, I suspect. The amount of wood that is actually consumed varies, with some animals accumulating a pile of chippings on the ground below the fence rail, while others swallow so much that they form bowel blockages which bring potentially disastrous consequences.

It is possible for a committed wood-chewer to munch his or her way through considerable amounts of wood in one sitting. When consumption reaches five kilograms (11 lbs) a day, it has to be said that the behaviour is far from normal. The relationship between wood-chewing and social isolation has been hinted at by the outstanding American equine behaviourist, Katherine Houpt. She reports the story of two ponies housed for a journey in a transporter that separated them from one another. By the end of the journey, there was a hole in the chipboard divider big enough for them to nuzzle and groom one another as nature had intended.

Other research has looked at the relationship between different diets and the frequency of wood-chewing. These studies suggest that diets that are low in fibre are likely to increase the prevalence of the unwelcome behaviour. So wood-chewing may be seen as a remedial step taken by some horses to boost the fibre content of their diets.

The prevalence of wood-chewing in horses at grass seems to follow a seasonal pattern, with a peak being reported in late winter, as if there is something missing from the grass at this time. Further research is needed to identify the dietary deficiencies in these cases and to improve our understanding of how the horse's body detects them.

Question
My three-year-old Connemara filly has taken to chewing the door frame of her stable. She has been lightly backed, but is currently out of work because we are concentrating on her older half-brother. I have tried taste deterrents but she really seems to have taught herself to enjoy rather than avoid the flavour of the bitter paint. I feel rather guilty. Will she turn into a crib-biter if I fail to prevent her from doing it?

Answer
The most important facts that we have to establish about any horse showing this behaviour revolve around diet. If you are limiting the amount of hay she receives, this could be the most important point to address before continuing with any further taste-deterrent experiments. A native breed of her age in light work can thrive on ad lib forage alone, as long as vitamin and mineral supplements are also made available. In other words, do not feed concentrates if this means that her access to forage becomes restricted.

The other key fact that needs to be established is the time of day that your filly is chewing. This may well tie in with her running out of hay and may serve as extra confirmation of the nature of the craving she is expressing. When you offer ad lib hay you can minimise waste and maintain her enthusiasm and motivation to feed by giving it to her in a hay-lage net, or simply reduce the size of the apertures in one hay net by placing it inside another.

For youngstock that are stabled it can also be especially helpful to offer gorse and root vegetables. Your filly is still experimenting with new features in her environment, so allowing her access to these varieties of plant matter will direct her exploratory interest and extra oral needs towards them rather than towards her door frame.

Given that Highland ponies have been bred to withstand the rigours of a Scottish winter, it may be prudent to ask yourself whether it is absolutely imperative that she comes into her stable at all. Furthermore, there is the question of whether or not she is brought in on her own. Social isolation can play a part in the development of this unwelcome behaviour, and so you may well improve matters if you can provide her with more visual and tactile company in the shape of equine neighbours.

No confirmed link between wood-chewing and crib-biting has been made. Although they both indicate high oral needs, they involve such completely different anatomical manoeuvres that any link between the two is bound to be a rather tenuous one. Furthermore, unlike crib-biting, wood-chewing can be performed sequentially in different sites, and so is not sufficiently invariant to be defined as a sterotypic behaviour pattern.

Z

Zoos

Zoos are assuming an increasingly important role in the conservation of endangered wildlife, and some of their most resounding successes have been in the field of equid breeding programmes. The disappearance of appropriate habitats continues to threaten restocking programmes that aim to return captive-bred stock to the wild.

One example is Przewalski's horses which are undergoing a programme of reintroduction into the wild. Drawn from an original population of only thirteen, the captive collections of these Mongolian natives have proved very interesting as specimens of true wild horses. However, survey results and data deriving from these groups of animals should be interpreted with caution: before applying their behaviour to our understanding of the way horses have evolved to perform, we must bear in mind that captivity itself may have changed the way innate behaviour patterns are expressed. Furthermore, the possibility of inbreeding should also prompt caution. Although zoo authorities go to great lengths to mix Przewalski's horses from collections all over the world, the fact that there were only thirteen animals in the first instance means that the gene pool is horribly shallow. Infanticide is reported in Przewalski's stallions and, despite its low prevalence, this phenomenon is intriguing to students of equine behaviour. However, there are those who argue that it has little significance because of the confinement and the general environmental limitations in zoos. Above all, many would agree that the Przewalski results cannot be applied to *Equus caballus* because, strictly speaking, they are not the same species.

APPENDIX

The Equine Behaviour Study Circle

For those readers who would be interested to learn more about horse behaviour, a small and very friendly society exists for that express purpose. Founded by Moira Williams, a celebrated horsewoman and professional psychologist, this worldwide non-profit-making association brings together researchers, veterinary surgeons, behaviourists, riding instructors and hobby riders via a twice-yearly journal. This magazine acts as an informal forum for the discussion of training methods, ethological concepts, anecdotes and curiosities. Editorial comment is offered by a recognised behavioural scientist, but the accent is on sharing information rather than expounding theories.

Anyone can join this independent organisation by writing to Olwen Way, the circle's secretary, at Grove Cottage, Brinkley, Newmarket, Suffolk, CB8 0SF.

ASSOCIATION OF PET
BEHAVIOUR COUNSELLORS

Association of Pet Behaviour Counsellors

At various points in this book I have referred to this association, which was founded in 1989 and now comprises over thirty member practices throughout the United Kingdom and four in the United States as well. Although primarily concentrating on canine and feline cases, the association has a number of members with experience of equine behavioural problems. These individuals can be contacted by writing to the association's secretary at the address below. All APBC members accept cases exclusively on referral from veterinary surgeons, and if after reading *Why Does My Horse . . . ?* you feel that you require more detailed and personal advice, contact your vet with a view to being referred to your nearest APBC equine clinic.

A full list of APBC clinics is available on request, and details of the numerous publications by APBC members can also be obtained by writing to the Hon. Secretary, Association of Pet Behaviour Counsellors, 257 Royal College Street, London NW1 9LU.

INDEX